# BOREN'S BLOCK ONE:

## — A SINKING SHIP —

*by Sidney S. Andrews*

ISBN: 1-4499-0629-X
EAN: 978-1-4499-0629-0


Edited by Kris Fulsaas
Graphic Design by Lori Fulsaas
Cover photo by Meryl Schenker

# CONTENTS

# PROLOGUE: GRAVITY

In time, molehills become mountains become molehills. Humanity builds its creations subject to nature's mandate—that is, by imperfect means with imperfect materials on imperfect foundations. Layer upon layer, we keep adding fallible substance to our molehills until our cumulative faults become so unsustainable that they yield to the benefit of gravity.

The rubble-laden molehill left behind by the mountain's collapse becomes the flawed foundation of the next mountain, which will succumb in a similar way—and so on. Evolution is the natural outcome of these cycles, since the methods and materials are improved in each iteration.

The native tribes of the Pacific Northwest view the cycles of life and death in much the same way. Death is a cyclical event wherein one form is exchanged for another in the movement from pure flesh to pure spirit. When one form's imperfections accumulate to the point of instability, wicked gravity takes hold and the life is transformed—or evolves—to permit entrance into the spirit world.

The protagonist of this story, Boren's Block One, is a small parcel of land in Seattle's Pioneer Square, and though one rarely ascribes human characteristics to real estate, this particular piece of ground cannot be dismissed as inanimate. From the moment of its birth—that is, when it became identified as a separate legal entity apart from the surrounding woods—the distinction between owner and owned has never been clear. Alas, it is as if the land has never truly belonged to any man.

This parcel is a tortured and cursed lot upon which many men built their dreams, and despite the absence of grave serial errors on their part, each man eventually found his construct deeply flawed. The succession of men who served as steward for this, our protagonist parcel, paid dearly for their affair, a result not only of actions they took and didn't take but also of the steady interference from what would seem to be disconnected forces and events. Someone or something always seemed to interfere with any attempted quiet enjoyment of this sorry lot. Although the methods and materials kept improving with each new dream, for some reason every collapse on this particular molehill was more disastrous than the one before. The only thing evolving in this place is tragedy.

Gravity's pull seems just a little stronger here.

# Introduction: Trivia

Sharks aren't interested in trivia. They swim about, circling and smelling, while the entirety of their being is directed toward a single objective: to eat. Real estate brokers are really no different—except their energies are focused on fees rather than food. Of course, reputation, personal integrity, and the like are important for a broker, but only to the extent that these traits relate to the continued collection of commissions. Sharks and their food, brokers and their fees, politicians and their reelection are all partners in the same myopia, with an eye on the prize instead of the process. Most unknowingly live largely joyless lives—save the thrill of the kill.

My association with Boren's Block One began in 1985, when I formed my real estate brokerage company, Commonwealth, on a shoestring and a mountain of obligations I had no ability to keep. With but one year spent in the real estate business, I was young, inexperienced, and wonderfully ignorant of the path that lay before me. My first career as a tax accountant offered little in the way of enlightenment, save the exception of witnessing firsthand how deep a financial hole one could potentially dig.

My co-founder and vice president, J. Allen, was our office-leasing czar; he had, only twelve months before, left the domestic steel industry that was taking its inexorable dive into obscurity. He was a practiced salesman, but his real estate experience was as limited as mine. We were both married, under thirty years of age, and hungry for financial success.

At the time of Commonwealth's inception, my friend Douglas Graham was a tenured salesman at the oldest real estate brokerage firm in Seattle. He was gregarious and personable, traits highly suitable for a professional whose stock in trade was "cold calling" wealthy individuals to advise them that he, and only he, could secure them the most favorable terms for a property. His specialty was investment sales—that is, the buying and selling of commercial land and buildings—a discipline that was as yet unrepresented at my company. Despite the relative inexperience of Commonwealth's principals, Graham nonetheless agreed to come on board to enjoy our friendship as well as the favorable financial terms we offered him. He was six years older than we were, and his years in the real estate business had given him a broad knowledge of all the relevant trivia about which we, sadly, had no clue—things such as industry customs and practices, reputations of others in the investment and brokerage community, and the phone numbers of the more serious real estate players in town. He was a good fit.

During this second career of mine, as a real estate broker, I wasn't much concerned with trivia either. However, as the years have passed—during my glacially slow evolution from shark to recovering fee addict—the bulk of my time has been spent on work avoidance and the pursuit of arcane knowledge that might help me and maybe, one day, somebody else. I scan my morning paper each day in the hope of uncovering some bright piece of trivia to color one of the many dark spots of my universal understanding. History, geology, and other formerly irrelevant subjects—aka fun facts—now enrich my postretirement days.

{  TRIVIA
   At the junction of the three main roads that led into ancient Rome, peasants on their way in and out of the great city would meet and talk about the issues of importance in their lives. However, Rome's patricians and noblemen assumed that the conversations at this junction—the *tri-via* (Latin for three roads)—were of no consequence because of the speakers. Hence, information that someone deemed unimportant became known as *trivia*.

## LAUNCHING A COMPANY

In what J. Allen and I would later realize was not the miracle we thought at the time, our little brokerage firm was retained by a group, led by some attorneys from California, to lease the celebrated Smith Tower, a forty-story terra-cotta marvel that had been built by typewriter magnate L. C. Smith in 1914. These lawyers had just bought the Seattle landmark—once known as the tallest building west of the Mississippi—primarily for tax reasons and sought the exposure and coddling only a Pioneer Square brokerage firm like Commonwealth could offer to fill the tower's many vacant spaces. We knew we were *that* brokerage firm and felt this high-profile assignment just might launch our careers to the dizzying heights that our fathers had always expected of us. So after swimming, circling, and smelling a bit, the erstwhile steel salesman and tax accountant decided to open a second real estate office in the Smith Tower.

At one of Graham's first sales meetings, Allen lamented the fact that parking for the would-be Smith Tower tenants was a major stumbling block in his fee generation efforts. Landmark buildings often suffer from this problem—what the industry terms functional obsolescence—because finding a parking spot in 1914 was not the problem it became in 1986. The prospective tenants were at the mercy of often-unscrupulous parking-lot operators, who would guarantee them nothing more than what the next thirty days would bring. Luxuries such as validation for clients' cars and employee parking were a roll of the dice.

Tenants can also be like sharks, overlooking important historical and aesthetic trivia in the selfish pursuit of practical advantages—such as where to park their cars. Because Graham's calendar was far from full, we decided to put him on the task of finding convenient parking for the tenants of our Smith Tower owners, who, in their sharklike zeal for passive losses and investment tax credits, had overlooked this incredibly significant piece of trivia.

Luckily, the solution was obvious to even the laziest of brokers, and in 1986, on behalf of our California clients, Commonwealth served as broker in the sale of the parking garage across the street to the west of the Smith Tower—the infamous structure known as the "Sinking Ship" Garage.

Immediately upon receipt of our commission check, we were fired as the leasing agent of the tower.

Our termination was not due to any action or inaction on our part, but a result of external events that had nothing to do with us. In light of our abrupt removal just six months into our "miracle" assignment, one might think we would have been disappointed. However, all things considered, our affair with the Smith Tower and the Sinking Ship Garage had gone pretty well.

But I'm getting ahead of myself ...

## LAUNCHING THE SINKING SHIP GARAGE

For those who have never seen it, this parking garage got its nickname from the fact that the structure, not surprisingly, actually does resemble a sinking ship. Sited on a sloping, triangular piece of land, the "bow" of the garage points westward, rising a full three stories above street level and, just like a large passenger liner, the "freeboard" is capped with tubular metal railings on both the port and starboard sides. Following the slope uphill to the east (or aft), the levels gradually disappear into the ground until finally sinking "underwater" into the street at the very eastern end of the garage (Second Avenue), to provide automobile access to the rooftop level.

Because the site actually rises in elevation from west to east, some think the garage's sinking appearance is merely an optical illusion, but if you have ever stood in it or upon it, wicked gravity makes it abundantly clear that the floors are steeply sloped from bow to stern. The garage designers ably recognized two things: first, the site had not the dimensions large enough to accommodate the dizzying circular drives used in today's multilevel garages, and second, the grade change was not of a magnitude great enough to permit street-level entry to four different levels. The natural grade might have allowed three stories, but the architects, like all good sharks, wanted more—always more—so they smartly decided to slope the floor plates to create the gradient that would allow all four floors to be accessed from street level.

It is the garage's decided tilt that really sells the sinking-ship effect. In fairness to the much-maligned architect, this was a fairly creative solution to an all-too-common problem. In fairness to all those who view it, the structure is perhaps the ugliest pile of concrete on the planet. Not a single attempt was made nor was a solitary penny spent to ameliorate its bulk, its disharmony with its surrounds, or its complete lack of any aesthetic appeal whatsoever. It possesses a strictly utilitarian design—252 parking stalls in 73,720 square feet, a very efficient 300 square feet per stall on an irregular footprint—and has been universally despised since the day it was first moored.

## LAUNCHING A CIVIC REVOLT

In addition to the creation of instant urban blight, the shipwrights of the Sinking Ship Garage can also be credited with the birthing of an important civic movement. Built in 1961, the garage was constructed on the site of what was once Seattle's finest hotel, the appropriately named Hotel Seattle, located in the city's birthplace, an area now known as Pioneer Square. Five stories of sandstone and brick, the alternately named Seattle Hotel was one of the area's finest examples of the Romanesque style of architecture that rose from the ashes of the Great Seattle Fire of 1889. Built in 1890, the hotel was a grand symbol of Seattle's fierce resiliency in the face of a townwide tragedy, in addition to being the well-manicured hostess that greeted each and every visitor to knock at Seattle's front door.

But seventy years later, the venerable lady was summarily razed without question or quarter by a group of gas-guzzling sharks that sought only profit in the form of a parking garage. History and other trivia were not considerations. Besides providing safe harbor for wayward travelers to moor their weary cars, this monstrosity of a garage generated righteous public outrage toward a city that would permit a developer to raze such a handsome, historic structure in favor of this cement car cozy.

In 1960, the prevailing trends in architecture were beginning to favor more futuristic, sterile-looking structures that were fabricated from materials not found in nature. Designs tended to show little regard for human scale. Curtain-wall construction techniques and the sheer bulk of the soulless boxes struck a very sour note among the preservationists, and they rebelled, championing the unfashionable old buildings made of familiar materials such as wood, stone, and brick. They sought to preserve Pioneer Square's unique and architecturally significant collection of Richardsonian-Romanesque structures, the majority of which had been erected shortly after the Great Seattle Fire.

Indeed, this assortment of obsolete warehouses and manufacturing buildings was in grave and immediate danger, due to the uptown interests that sought and openly proposed to raze the buildings of Pioneer Square in favor of a paved paradise to serve as their parking lot. When a neighboring building at First and Yesler came down a few years after the Seattle Hotel, the peasants finally revolted. In 1970, the fifty-two-acre Pioneer Square Historic District was created and listed on the National Register of Historic Places, which protected the brick dinosaurs by way of a local land-use ordinance and a stakeholder-run Preservation Board to oversee the use and adaptive reuse of the roughly thirty blocks of nineteenth-century relics. Yet the ordinance was too late to change the fate of the Hotel Seattle.

## IS THE SINKING SHIP GARAGE SUNK?

So in autumn 2004, when I read in my morning paper that the Sinking Ship Garage was again in the news, my trivia gland twitched. Because I had brokered a sale of the beast back in 1986, I was familiar with the garage and many of the players in the drama. The newspaper story, which chronicled the legal battle being waged between owner HTK Management LLC (HTK) and municipal transit authority Seattle Popular Monorail Authority (known as the Seattle Monorail Project, or SMP), explained that the nature of the fight hinged on the scope and proper application of the sovereign power of eminent domain. This was an important and precedent-setting case, and the Washington State Supreme Court would soon be deliberating its merits.

SMP, whose mandate was to build a fourteen-mile monorail system elevated above the city streets, was seeking to condemn the 20,000-square-foot site because it wanted to locate a transit station there but ultimately needed only a fraction of the property for the station itself. The unneeded balance of the land was to be used by SMP for staging and related activities during construction of the monorail's so-called "Green Line" and then might later be further developed, leased, or sold for some unidentified redevelopment.

HTK had stipulated that it was willing to sell the land needed for the SMP station (roughly one-third of the site) but wished to retain the balance of the land once construction of the station was completed. HTK offered a temporary easement to SMP for the staging area, seeking to limit the condemnation to just the smaller station requirements, while SMP argued the need for the entire site upon which the Sinking Ship Garage rested—Lots One through Four of Block One, C. D. Boren's plat of the city of Seattle.

The decision makers at SMP included local real estate people, shrewd and experienced developers who were skilled at maximizing the value of a real estate holding. Well known to them was the real estate maxim that all boats float with a rising tide. Public investment begets urban renewal, which begets property appreciation, which in turn begets private investment. They were not concerned about acquiring more land than they needed for their Green Line, knowing full well that if and when the time came to sell any excess land, its after-improved market value would far exceed its cost. Private industry had always sought participation in adjacent property appreciation created as a result of their risk and investment, so why shouldn't a public agency?

In fact, contained in SMP's formally adopted development policies was a reference to something called "associated development," which was defined as a "freestanding project not connected with a (monorail) station, built by a third party on land that SMP has fee ownership (of) or development rights (to) and is most likely built after a station is built. The land could be sold outright or ground leased." Clearly, the unused balance of Boren's Block One was a prime candidate for such associated development, which likely would yield SMP a healthy profit once construction was completed. And (to revisit the marine metaphor one more time) this Sinking Ship, if left to stand, was one that would never rise with any tide ...

More subtext in this dispute, not detailed in the newspaper article but nonetheless a factor, hinged on the notion that the Sinking Ship Garage had been for nearly fifty years the proverbial tear in the historic fabric of Pioneer Square. Preservationists had unsuccessfully sought ways to rid this important block—it squats squarely on the front porch of Pioneer Square—of its unwelcome and unsightly occupant. In its legal briefs, SMP was always quick to point to the community support its condemnation action enjoyed, without really ever articulating why. The fact was that the local folks wanted this concrete embodiment of greed and avarice stricken from both their consciousness and their neighborhood. The community brought all its weight to bear on the city bureaucrats and SMP to help them in creating the perfect storm to fully and finally submerge the Sinking Ship. This triangle was a sorry and cursed lot, and the evidence of its past needed to go.

But this piece of land was not always an unwanted eyesore ...

# CHAPTER 1:

# MOLEHILLS

In 1850, the land that present-day Pioneer Square occupies was used by the Suquampsh (Suquamish) Indians for a small fishing camp. The camp came to be within the tribe's domain because its chief, whose main encampment was on the opposite shore of Puget Sound in present-day Suquamish, was the issue of a Suquampsh tyee and a Duwampsh (Duwamish) mother. His name was Sealth (Seattle). The Duwampsh hunting and fishing grounds consisted of this camp and the general environs surrounding what is now known as the Duwamish River, so Chief Seattle's ascendancy effectively merged the two tribes' ranges.

The chief's tribesmen were a most contented lot, owing mostly to the abundance of food available in and around the waters of Puget Sound. Consequently, they were also a relatively passive group, since aggression was for the most part unnecessary to keep their members fat and happy. The weather was mild, the waters were calm, and life was easy. In short, they were vulnerable.

## 1851: THE FIRST SETTLEMENT—ALKI POINT

In March 1852, when David Swinson "Doc" Maynard arrived in "New York–Alki" (pronounced "AL-key," from native jargon meaning "soon") at present-day Alki Point, two dozen men, women, and children had resided there about five months in a handful of log cabins. Within this settlement of twenty-four, one faction led by a man named Arthur Denny decided that their fortunes would be made not in their previous vocation as farmers, but as timber men and traders.

Arthur Denny, born June 20, 1822, in Washington County, Indiana, was the fourth of eight sons of John and Sarah Wilson Denny. He was, like his father, a staunch supporter of the Whig party, a pious member of the Methodist Episcopal Church, and an unwavering man of temperance. A disciplined and serious man, he behaved strictly in accordance with church doctrine and expected the same from those around him. Denny's mother, Sarah Wilson Denny, died when Arthur was eighteen years old, and he later recorded that the care and custody of his dying mother was the single most important act of his life. Before coming west, he married Mary Ann Boren, the eldest daughter of Richard Freeman Boren and Sarah Latimer Boren, and held the office of official surveyor for Knox County, Illinois.

At Alki Point, the Denny party correctly deduced that its shallow water and wicked exposure to wind and weather made it not the ideal place to birth a great seaport from which to sell their logs. Furthermore, another of the twenty-four settlers, Lee Terry, had arrived before Denny's group and had already made known his designs on the sandy point by naming it New York–Alki after his hometown in the great state of New York. Thus, the Denny party decided to remove themselves from the prominent jetty to a suitably protected deep-water port where the bounty of the great Northwest could be sold and delivered at a profit.

## The Second Settlement: Chief Seattle's Land

To Arthur Denny's eye, just northeast of the nearby Duwamish River mouth lay such a site, combining protection from the elements— provided by Duwamish Head to the south and West Point to the north—and water depths too great to be measured with the clothesline and horseshoe sounding rig Denny's group had devised. As a result of these observations, Arthur Denny, Carson Boren, and William Bell were certain that they wished to make their claim on the eastern shore of Elliott Bay and immediately set about doing so, splitting up the deep-water frontage of what the natives called Duwampsh equally among themselves. Terry and his group, which weren't particularly fond of the others anyway, stayed put on Alki. Boren, Denny, and Bell agreed that their 320-acre donation land claims would begin at what is now King Street and run as far north as today's Denny Way. These adjacent claims would be rectangular in shape, with the short sides fronting the shoreline. The new settlement's location was settled, and all that remained to do was the formality of filing the claims and moving onto the land.

Doc Maynard and his arrival on the scene now threw a wrench in the works, in more ways than one. Maynard was a democrat, a doctor, and a drinker, which made him oil to Denny's water. Born in Vermont, he had come west from Ohio in 1850 to escape an unrewarding marriage to a woman named Lydia Rickey, whom he alleged some years later was sleeping with every man in Cleveland but him. In his journey to the Oregon Territory by wagon train, he became enamored with a widow by the name of Catherine Broshears, and the pursuit of her affection consumed a significant part of the next two years of his life. For reasons likely related to the fact that marriage doubled the potential size of a donation land claim, Maynard postponed the official truncation of his original matrimonial affliction to Lydia until he found sufficient legal cause to do so, an engaging story that is well documented in most of Seattle's historical tomes. His subsequent marriage to the widow Broshears was, however, apparently not deemed by Doc to be sufficient cause for divorcing his first wife, so Maynard became King County's first bigamist by virtue of this indiscretion. He was, in short, a colorful character.

He had also entered into a partnership with the noble Suquamish tyee—tall, broad-cheeked Seattle—whereby the tribe would catch a fortune in salmon and Maynard would in turn salt it away in barrels to be sold in San Francisco. A fine plan it was, but there was a problem: Doc had neither wharf nor port—nor even a barrel, for that matter. Fortunately for Maynard, party leader Denny was victimized by what a nineteenth-century man called the ague, or malarial fever, which rendered him useless on a far too regular basis. The wily Dr. Maynard carried a little black bag full of wonderful tricks, two of which happened to be opium and alcohol—for medicinal purposes only, of course. It was the perfect pioneer barter. Doc tended to Denny's ague with the tools of his trade, and Denny solved Maynard's real estate problem. The new settlement was in need of a good doctor, and Denny persuaded the others to make Maynard feel welcome by shifting their claims northward so as to carve out some deep-water frontage at the south end for Doc. There was plenty of shoreline and even more land, so at the time this seemed to them a small accommodation. The nascent settlement was then resettled.

The mercurial and mischievous Maynard recorded his claim in the area that includes what we call today Pioneer Square and the International District, laying out his plat consistent with the Organic Act—that is, the streets running true to the four major points of the compass. Being a practical man, this layout also made perfect sense to him, since the boundaries of his claim ran true to the same four compass points, and the shoreline on his land also ran north to south. Thus, his Commercial Avenue (now First Avenue South) paralleled the beach, with the cross streets running perpendicular thereto. The claim featured nearly 300 yards of deep-water frontage, a peninsula roughly two blocks wide extending southerly from Yesler Way to King Street, an upland lagoon east of the peninsula, and a sizable amount of what was thought to be unusable marshes and hill behind. So-called Maynard's Point marked the southern tip of the peninsula and stood some thirty feet above the high tide mark, solemnly witnessing the mighty Duwamish River spill into Elliott Bay.

The only native use of the parcel was a fishing camp that was located just east of the "sag" at the foot of present-day Yesler Way, where the land bowed gracefully to meet the water—so much so that Maynard's Point was actually an island at high tide as the tidewaters rushed through the sag to meet the lagoon behind the peninsula. The camp was in a perfect position to catch the hordes of fat salmon returning home to spawn as well as to observe all the comings and goings of the various upstream tribes—some of which were not friendly to Chief Seattle. Fortunately for Doc, this camp belonged to his friend (and partner), Chief Seattle, who was more than happy to share it with him.

The idea that Doc had made the deal for his claim with a highly medicated Denny, a devout Methodist teetotaler, while he was pickled on Doc's booze and opium is a most attractive theory indeed. Doc was a cunning sort and, of the four claims, Maynard's possessed the most easily developable and, hence, valuable land, owing to the absence of towering bluffs where the land meets the sea. Boren's claim had reasonable grades, but Denny and Bell were both confronted with considerable grade and bluff. This intoxicating notion may have played some role in Denny's largesse, but other factors may have been in operation as well.

Interestingly enough, at the time of filing of the donation claims in 1853, there was no treaty with the local Indians—not until 1855—and it would not be inaccurate to assert that the U.S. government, in giving the settlers their land claims, was gifting territory it did not own. Additionally, by government rules, the way for settlers to perfect their land claims was to erect a structure upon it—that is, ownership was not conclusively established until there was claimant investment and some tangible evidence of ownership visible to the transient world. It stands to reason that Denny might have been encouraged to give this parcel to Maynard since, legally and practically, its white ownership was in doubt owing to the lack of a binding treaty with the locals, combined with the natives' obvious use of the property through the existence of their fishing lodge. So he gave this molehill—land he did not and perhaps could not own—to Maynard.

## Two Platting Philosophies Yield an Awkward Grid

Directly to the north of Maynard's plat was the claim of Carson Boren, a 320-acre rectangle beginning at Yesler Way. Surveyor Arthur Denny, who was also Boren's brother-in-law, laid out Boren's plat similarly to his own—that is, locating the streets with the highest regard for the natural shape of the shoreline, which minimized the impact of the imposing hills behind. Since the shoreline north of Yesler meanders not insignificantly to the west, Denny's Front Street (now First Avenue) had a decided westerly tilt relative to Maynard's Commercial Avenue, which made a simple meeting of the streets impossible without one side yielding to the other.

Try as he might, Denny had no success trying to dissuade Doc from his platting plan. Maynard's mind was made up, and yielding was not part of the plan. Maynard even refused to bend the streets at the north end of his claim so as to permit continuity between plats, which was the first round in a long history of acrimony between the two men. Denny explained the situation in his book *Pioneer Days on Puget Sound*: "The Doctor, who occasionally stimulated himself a little, that day had taken enough to feel that he was not only monarch of all he surveyed but what Boren and I surveyed as well."

It could be said that platting is a two-way street, since Denny also refused to bend, his streets or otherwise. Roughly thirty degrees separated the layout of the north-south streets, and for anyone who had to deal with the confusion, this was a significant slice of pie. In fact, one parcel of land—Boren's Block One—was exactly that piece of pie, a triangular remnant wedged right between the considerable wills of Arthur Armstrong Denny and David Swinson Maynard. That piece of pie at the junction of three roads leading into the heart of ancient Seattle, a once-happy little fishing lodge just east of the sag, was already suffering under the new regime.

{ ARTHUR DENNY: SEATTLE'S FIRST SURVEYOR
Arthur Denny was a skilled surveyor, and while rights-of-way could have any orientation the settlers desired, the perimeter of the donation claims were required to run only north, south, east, and west. This created a most interesting situation for Denny, since the shoreline in front of both his and Carson Boren's claims ran northwest to southeast. Denny and Boren could either run the northern boundary line to the shore, which re-

sulted in retaining all the waterfront but located a good chunk of the claim underwater at the southern end, or begin the southern boundary of the rectangle at the shore, which maximized the dry acreage but yielded just a few blocks of waterfront.

Surely, it was a prickly dilemma. One can only imagine the conversations around the fire at night, but apparently Boren was convinced by Denny that giving up his waterfront was in his best interest—presumably because Boren preferred farmland to tideland. A good thing, since Denny was the lucky recipient of this waterfront, which gave his claim a shape similar to that of a woodpecker's head, with the beak being the waterfront in front of Boren's claim. Obviously, Denny was not persuaded by the same argument that he used to sway Boren, because he chose to keep all his waterfront—and Boren's too.

## THE BOREN BUNCH: TANGLED GENEALOGIES

Carson Dobbins Boren, or "Uncle Dobbins," as he was called, was a skilled hunter and outdoorsman. He was born in 1824, the first son of Richard and Sarah Latimer Boren and the younger brother of Mary Ann, later Arthur Denny's wife. Father Richard was a cabinetmaker who disappeared mysteriously and completely from the public records sometime in the late 1820s. The only evidence of his whereabouts and his fate is a story recounted by Richard's granddaughter, Emily Inez Denny, some seventy years later. The granddaughter, Arthur and Mary Ann Boren Denny's daughter, reported the following in her book, *Blazing the Way*, as told to her by her grandmother Sarah Latimer Boren (later Denny):

> She [Sarah Latimer] soon married Richard Freeman Boren, whose conversion and call to the ministry were clear and decided. While yet in apparently perfect health he disposed of all his [cabinet-making] tools, saying that he would not need them any more. One night, toward morning, she dreamed that she saw a horse saddled and bridled at the gate and some one said to her that she must mount and ride to see her husband, who was very sick; she obeyed, in her dream, riding over a strange road, crossing a swollen stream at one point. At daylight she awoke; a horse with

sidesaddle on was waiting and a messenger called her to go to her husband, as he was dangerously ill at a distant house. Exactly as in her dream she was conducted, she traversed the road and crossed the swollen stream to reach the place where he lay, stricken with a fatal malady.

It is clearly a story of a man fondly remembered; however, to an objective observer, it would seem, in the best case, irresponsible for a nineteenth-century man with a wife and three young children to abruptly liquidate the implements of his livelihood and ride off into the sunset in some frothy evangelical fervor—not to mention downright discourteous to die shortly thereafter. History has recorded just a dream and some "fatal malady" in an undisclosed location to rationalize his disappearance, but more cynical minds could surely devise other explanations.

Carson Boren wed Mary Ann Kays in Knox County, Illinois, on February 18, 1849, and, sadly, it was not a blessed union. Dissatisfied with home life and city life upon his arrival west, he kept moving farther away from Seattle as the years went by, deeper and deeper into the woods, until finally passing this earth in 1912 at the ripe old age of eighty-eight on his ranch in present-day Woodinville. He is the most underreported settler of the bunch, with most notable Seattle historians giving little, if any, mention of his contributions (*The History of Seattle*, Clarence Bagley's 1,100-page three-volume tome, has less than one-half page dedicated to the life and lessons of Carson Boren in a paragraph that is warmly titled "The Boren Family." It lists only names and dates and is completely devoid of the flowery biographical remembrances showered upon the hundreds of other pioneers it lists). Boren even lost sole name recognition on his own claim, as the county records soon began to refer to his claim as the Boren and Denny Addition to the Town of Seattle instead of the original "C. D. Boren's Plat."

It would not stretch the imagination to think that perhaps Boren was not particularly close to his extended family, nor is there much evidence to support the notion that he and Denny were close.

Uncle Dobbins was not only Arthur Denny's brother-in-law (by virtue of Arthur's marriage to Boren's sister Mary Ann) but also his
stepbrother (on account of the marriage of Denny's father, John, to
Boren's mother, Sarah, after she was—presumably—widowed). Carson Boren and Arthur Denny spent seven tortuous months together
in wagons traveling the dangerous and difficult trail to the Puget
Sound country, most of this time with Arthur, who—helpless and
ague-stricken—from his sickbed purported to be the leader. Boren
helped build Denny's cabins on both Alki and Elliott Bay while Denny, sick again, was bedridden (both of which an ungrateful Denny
quickly abandoned—because of poor site selection—and moved on
to Boren's land at First and Marion). For Denny's part, his unyield-
ing puritan principles no doubt frowned on Boren's estrangement
from his wife; for Boren, the waterfront real estate debacle must have
been a source of considerable embarrassment. Maybe the two men
were just a little bit too closely aligned by adjoining land claims and
intermingled families.

The Denny-Boren party left Knox County, Illinois, in April 1851
and reached the shores of Alki in November of the same year. Allegedly, Arthur was named captain of the train in Illinois, but his
persistent incapacity necessitated a replacement, which was ably assumed by his battle-hardened father, John Denny. Devout Methodist, staunch Whig, and prolific breeder, John Denny had eight sons
by his first wife, Sarah Wilson Denny—the names of said progeny
being Lewis, Alford, John, Arthur, James, Samuel, David, and Allen
(aka Wiley). John Denny married his second wife, Sarah Latimer
Boren, in 1848 and fathered daughter Loretta at age 57 (Sarah was
45) six weeks before coming west. The elder three Denny brothers stayed behind in Illinois, while John and Sarah (with six-week
old Loretta), Arthur and Mary Ann (with two young daughters,
Louisa Catherine and Margaret Lenora), and the four younger unmarried Denny brothers began the long and arduous adventure on
the Oregon Trail with the Boren clan—Carson, his wife, Mary Ann
(with infant daughter Gertrude), and his unmarried sister Louisa

(soon to be Mrs. David Denny). They were the nineteenth-century traveling version of the Brady Bunch, only in this case, Greg, Marsha, and the rest of the Brady kids all married each other.

The notion of intermarrying was not foreign to the Boren clan, as various researchers have substantiated. Although the records are not extensive, what data does exist indicates that the MacIntosh and Boren families traveled and frequently procreated together in the hills of Kentucky and Tennessee during the eighteenth and early nineteenth centuries; if these records are accurate, Borens have on occasion been known to marry Borens. Historians within the Boren family have not repudiated this, and large portions of the Boren family tree were followers of Joseph Smith and the newly founded Mormon Church.

The Boren family was not alone in its ties to the Mormon Church. John Denny was a member of the Illinois Legislature that in 1841 gave authority to Smith, the Mormon founder and prophet, to preempt federal and state laws and rule his settlement in Nauvoo, Illinois, as if it were his personal fiefdom via a liberal city charter that granted broad habeas corpus powers to the local court. Through these powers, Smith was able to escape extradition to the many states in which he had previously settled and ran afoul of the law, which only served to fan the flames of resentment toward the Mormons. Methodists (such as the Dennys) were much more sympathetic to the plight of the Mormons—more so than the other Christian denominations—and many of Smith's converts came from the Methodist ranks.

As John Denny captained the family wagon train west, his last stop before crossing the Missouri River was Kanesville, Iowa, a Mormon settlement just east of the river. Kanesville was established in 1847 as a wintering ground for the substantial migration of Joseph Smith's followers as they moved from the persecution and bloodshed in Illinois through the Rocky Mountains to, ultimately, the Great Salt Lake in Utah. Denny's wagon train was welcomed at Kanesville and provisioned for the crossing of the vast and dangerous prairie land that lay ahead.

What would possess John Denny, a distinguished fifty-eight-year-old man with a new wife and six-week-old daughter, to abandon his home, a notable career, and much of his family to face the dust, disease, and death of the Oregon Trail? What motivated Richard Freeman Boren to quit his job and become a traveling pastor? Did he really die, as his granddaughter suggests in the dream scenario, or did he meet another fate (for instance, leaving his family to join a Mormon missionary as had Oliver Cowdery, who was spreading Mormon doctrine and tales of Smith's golden tablets of Moroni at the time)? Was the Denny family influenced by the burgeoning Mormon Church (Knox County was a stone's throw from Nauvoo), heading west to avoid persecution and found a new Mormon settlement? Is it simply coincidence that the two wives of John Denny were named Sarah and that the children each chose their stepsiblings as mates?

Taken as a whole, the set of facts are quite extraordinary—and, in some cases, bordering on fantastic. Sadly, those in a position to know the answers were stoic and chose not to acknowledge the questions. Some twenty different stories with forty separate endings could be spun from the very limited publicly verifiable information available in this saga. Perhaps this is just an amazing series of oddities and coincidences, but I wonder, does anyone else hear the *Deliverance* banjo?

## THE NORTHWEST'S FIRST STEAM SAWMILL

In October 1852, six months after Maynard appeared on the scene, an Ohioan by the name of Henry L. Yesler arrived in town. He and partner John Stroble had spent the past several months scouting all points north of Portland for a suitable spot to locate a steam sawmill. No other town on Puget Sound had a *steam* sawmill yet, hence the competition for Yesler's project was intense. Since the Puget Sound town with the most toys would surely rise to Northwest supremacy, free land and the key to the city were offered to Stroble and Yesler in every settlement from Olympia to Grays Harbor. Hell, the Terry brothers at Alki offered him the whole damn point.

The ideal site for a steam-powered sawmill included plenty of level ground adjacent to deep water, with an ample supply of standing timber easily accessible to the mill and attendant wharf. Fortunately, it turned out that Maynard's "sag" was exactly such a place, and Doc, in a giving mood just like the three men before him, felt this to be a small accommodation. Yesler got his level land, his deep water, and his access to the millions of board feet of timber that stood on the forested hills above; thus, the town that would become Seattle got the steam sawmill.

The Yesler name is very quiet in the history books shortly after his much-ballyhooed arrival in Seattle because partner Stroble pulled out of the project early, leaving an incompetent and inexperienced Yesler to build and manage an operation that was clearly beyond him. Most all of the early residents of Seattle worked a spell in the mill—Arthur Denny, David Denny, Carson Boren, and Lewis Wyckoff among them—but all these stints were short-lived, as was Yesler's ownership of the mill, since he, time has shown, was not the sharpest blade in the mill.

The access and later "skid road" to Yesler's mill, Mill Street, split the Maynard and Boren claims, serving as the mediator between two stubborn waterfront streets, Maynard's Commercial Avenue and Denny's Front Street. Yesler's mill and wharf were sited on the choicest parcel at the northern end of Maynard's plat, owing in no small part to Doc's unfailing optimism and largesse. Boren was convinced to chip in as well and deeded to Yesler a sizable parcel of land, including Lots One through Four of Boren's Block One. (Although the Maynard, Denny, Boren, and Bell claims weren't recorded until May 1853, the locations of the claims had already been settled—twice, in fact—thus Yesler never got his name on this plat).

In what could be recognized as Arthur Denny's real estate savvy (or, more likely, dumb luck), the settlement clustered on either side of Boren's Block One, patterning an American urban layout that was repeated time and time again in cities around the country—that is, with the industrial and commercial section to the south (on Maynard's plat) and the residential areas to the north (on Boren's land). Mill Street (now Yesler Way) was the line of division, or the Deadline, as it was later called. Boren, Denny, Yesler, and their ilk all lived above (north of) the line, while the mill, boardinghouses, and Indian camps were all below (south of) the line. This left Maynard with the responsibility of letting the new arrivals (who had little or no money) settle on his land, which he freely did, while the others' claims were left largely untouched, waiting to be sold when prices improved in the growing town. This is one of the reasons Doc Maynard left this earth with nary a cent or deed to his name, as the land of his original claim was all given, bartered, sold, or squandered along the way. (Maynard eventually lost half his land when his first wife, Lydia, from whom he later obtained a divorce without her knowledge, suddenly arrived in Seattle to lay claim to her property. Bizarrely, while in Seattle she resided with her former husband and his new wife throughout the lengthy legal ordeal, which was resolved with a determination that half of his land belonged neither to husband nor wife nor first wife, but instead reverted to the government due to his duplicity.)

## 1856: THE BATTLE OF SEATTLE

Being in Seattle's swirling epicenter provided Boren's Block One the opportunity to bear witness to all of the young town's more violent events. Criminals were hung from a board that was suspended between two maple trees at the west end of Boren's Block One, but the most famous violence, the Battle of Seattle—the culmination of the Indian Wars of 1855-6—was also centered on our sorry little lot.

Understandably, when two diverse cultures are quickly thrown together, conflict trumps concord. The flood of white settlers pouring into the region was putting enormous pressure on the Indian way of life. Skirmishes were breaking out everywhere, and the violence was escalating all across what is now Washington State. Petty theft evolved into grand larceny as anxiety turned to fear; assault became murder as discomfort grew to rage. Thus, the events of January

26, 1856, should have come as no surprise when, after five years of poorly behaved white men behaving poorly, the native tribes gathered in Seattle for payback.

As the marauders massed in the tree-lined hills above the town, resident friendly Indians identified the foreigners' positions to the sailors onboard the U.S.S. *Decatur*, which was floating about a hundred yards offshore of Yesler's mill. The warship emptied the batteries of its cannons (and onshore howitzers) randomly into the anonymous forest for hours, while the Indians returned the favor with what little small-arms fire they could muster. The whites and friendly Indians—there were many—scurried into the blockade located in the north end of town at First and Cherry to watch the fireworks overhead.

Homes were pillaged and stores were plundered, but the casualty reports were always light, with none counting more than two whites among the victims. The men of the offshore *Decatur* proudly took credit for saving the lives of the wretched souls of Seattle from the heathens' rage and teaching the bloodthirsty savages a stern lesson in the hegemony of the great white chief.

{ LIEUTENANT PHELPS: ONE DAY'S WORK
One young officer of the U.S.S. *Decatur*, a certain Lieutenant Phelps, parlayed his heroism during the Battle of Seattle to such a degree that he soon gained entry into many Seattle history books with his account of the action as well as the title of Admiral of the U.S. Navy.

The number of Indian casualties in the battle was never recorded in any of the myriad historical accounts of the battle, but surely there must have been many. The Indian will was crushed, and the hillside that had once cradled the happy little fishing camp was now colored dark with the blood of the black-hearted braves. White supremacy had been firmly established, but at what cost?

The cost was not recorded in the history books either.

# Chapter 2:

# Mountains

During the first twenty years of the existence of Boren's Block One (since its evolution from a small fishing camp), the number and frequency of its conveyances stand in stark contrast to the very still path of the next one hundred years. Perhaps this speaks to the interest and excitement the parcel commanded in its infancy, or maybe it evidences the malaise ever since. But in any event, many now-familiar pioneer names took turns babysitting the wild child upon their arrival in Seattle.

## 1859: Henry Yesler Sells Boren's Block One to Lewis Wyckoff

Henry Yesler, in what may have been the single most intelligent act of his life, turned some of Maynard's and Boren's gifts into a tidy profit, including Boren's Block One, which he sold to town blacksmith, liveryman, sheriff, and tax assessor Lewis V. Wyckoff on May 28, 1859. Wyckoff was one of the first settlers to locate in the vicinity prior to the recordation of the earlier group's claims, and while his name is one that historians rarely cite, his appearance in the King County property records commands many pages. According to fellow explorer Arthur Denny, Wyckoff was also a member of the first official white party to blaze a trail and later a road over Snoqualmie Pass in the effort to hasten the advent of Seattle's designation as the northern terminus of the Northern Pacific Railroad.

## 1861: WYCKOFF MORTGAGES TO LUTHER COLLINS

Two years after he acquired Block One, Wyckoff granted a mortgage to Luther M. Collins to secure the former's indebtedness to the latter for the purchase of fourteen horses with saddles, a threshing machine, one fanning mill, twenty-one hogs, ten cattle, a wagon, plows, and other assorted farming implements. Luther Collins was a member of the first white party to arrive in the Seattle area but had the misfortune of choosing a vastly inferior area to settle. A farmer by trade, he first homesteaded on the Nisqually River around 1847 with three associates: Henry Van Asselt, Jacob Maple, and son Samuel Maple. However, finding themselves without much company, they relocated and selected claims on the Duwamish River in September 1851 (in present-day Georgetown), two months before the schooner *Exact* brought Boren, Bell, and Denny to the shores of Alki. Collins was well known around the Sound and brought fame and countless new settlers to the Duwamish valley by peddling his forty-pound cabbages and thirty-pound beets on the streets of Seattle.

Collins was a quintessential pioneer character, much like his friend Doc Maynard. When Maynard got his divorce from wife-in-absentia Lydia Rickey Maynard, it was Luther Collins who testified "that the evil disposition of his [Maynard's] wife" was sufficient cause for a divorce. Yet Collins and Lydia had never met. In return, Justice of the Peace Maynard repeatedly rescued Collins from himself and his constant legal troubles since Luther had a nasty habit of killing folks that he didn't like. Doc got two murder charges dropped against Collins and even managed to get him appointed as one of the original three King County Commissioners by the Oregon Legislature (which had jurisdiction at the time).

{   LUTHER COLLINS: PIONEER RULE OF LAW
    Luther Collins can be indirectly credited with whipping up the
    first law and order movement in lawless Seattle (a recurring
    theme throughout Seattle politics for the next fifty years). Lu-

ther was no milquetoast, and during his time among the natives, he developed unique methods of communicating with those whom he chose as neighbors—one of his more charming affectations being the tender habit of hanging on his fence posts the scalps of the last ten locals with whom he disagreed.

For some prurient reason, he and the Maple boys some years later took it upon themselves to dispense their own form of pioneer justice to a Duwamish Indian by the name of Massachie Jim for violence he allegedly inflicted on his squaw— they hung him. Jim's tribal members were not so upset with his demise (Massachie is Salish for "evil"), but when a white man turned up bludgeoned to death shortly thereafter, some folks felt this was an act of revenge and that all hell would break loose.

Foam frothed about the mouths of the god-fearing law and order bunch, so Territorial Supreme Court Judge Edward Lander quickly sprung into decisive action, demanding that all murderers found guilty, whether settlers or Indians, pay the ultimate penalty for their misdeeds. To no one's surprise, the all-white juries cleared Collins and his friends of any wrongdoing.

Regardless, Collins's loan to Wyckoff was promptly repaid, as evidenced by the mortgage being stamped "satisfied" within the year. A few months later, Collins drowned panning for gold in Idaho in 1862; Sheriff Wyckoff dropped dead suddenly in 1882 after a mob lynched two men from the maples in his former front yard—some say he was despondent over his failure to prevent the hanging.

## 1864: HENRY YESLER SELLS LOT ONE TO JOHN CONDON

Oddly, Yesler had withheld Lot One of Boren's Block One (the western point of the pie that hosted the above-mentioned maples) from Wyckoff in 1859, selling him only the eastern Lots Two, Three, and Four that front Second Avenue. Whether he wanted to better insulate his mill and residence (his home was just to the north), whether he enjoyed his gallows front row seat, or whether it was simply an unintentional defect in the deed, is unknown, but whatever Yesler's reason, it ceased to be germane five years later, as he deeded Lot One to one of Wyckoff's successors, Irish immigrant John S. Condon, on February 16, 1864.

## 1864: WYCKOFF SELLS TO CONDON, AMOS BROWN, AND MOSES MADDOCKS

John Condon and his business partners, Amos Brown and Moses Maddocks, presumably met in the logging camps of Port Gamble (Maddocks sold his Port Gamble logging company to Brown in 1863). This unlikely triumvirate—Scottish timber man Brown, Welsh builder Maddocks, and Irish entrepreneur Condon—found on their occasional business trips to Seattle that overnight accommodations for visiting businessmen were woefully inadequate, so they decided to fill the need.

They began by purchasing Lewis Wyckoff's land, Lots Two, Three, and Four of Boren's Block One, for $1,500, on February 16, 1864 (although Brown's interest never included a recorded deed for the property). Upon it they erected a thirty-room white clapboard house in the summer of 1864. Maddocks was in charge of the construction, Brown supplied the lumber, and Condon was the operations man. They named it the Occidental Hotel.

{ FELKER HOUSE: SEATTLE'S FIRST ACCOMMODATIONS

At the time the Occidental Hotel was built, the only civilized establishment available to visitors in Seattle was Felker House, owned by Captain Leonard Felker. Captain Felker and Doc Maynard had been business partners for years, beginning with Maynard's famous forest of a woodpile he had cut in Olympia during his long and difficult courtship of the widow Catherine Broshears. (Her brother strenuously objected to her cavorting with a married man, and the enormity of Maynard's Bunyanesque woodpile matched the depth of his despair.) Felker shipped Maynard's mile-high pile down to San Francisco and used the whopping $16,000 sales proceeds to purchase and deliver the inventory for Maynard's (and Seattle's first) mercantile store.

Felker earned Maynard's everlasting affection when he was able to pick up Maynard's goods for pennies on the dollar because the San Francisco longshoremen had, en masse, abandoned their jobs in the bum's rush for the California gold-fields. The ship captains, without anyone to unload their cargo, were eager to discharge their stranded goods to anyone who would take them, thus it was often sold by the captains for just the shipping charges due. In return, Maynard sold the Felker House lot for just $20. (Although recipients of a donation claim were technically unable to sell their land for five years, Maynard easily got around this.)

The most ingenious arrangement of the pair involved the first sale of property in Seattle—made before the original plats were filed—when Maynard sold Felker a lot near his store at First and Main. The curious part of this transaction was that this particular lot was underwater at least half the time—which was Doc's problem. Felker also had a problem, which was what to do with his ship's ballast (rocks and the like that filled the hold to steady an empty vessel at sea) from the brig *Franklin Adams*. Federal law prohibited dumping ballast into a harbor, so Doc and Felker created Seattle's first unofficial land-fill by charging cargo ships $5 a ton to dump their ballast on Felker's (and also Maynard's) tidelands—now known as Ballast Island (or Pier 48). Doc turned worthless beach into saleable lots, and Felker got to dump his ballast for free. (Ironically, the end result is that Seattle's waterfront from Yesler to King Street consists of, in considerable part, the top of Telegraph Hill in San Francisco.)

Built in 1853, Felker House was a grand Southern mansion that perched atop the most prominent site in town at Maynard's Point (First and Jackson, at present-day Merrill Place). The imported two-story structure delivered by Felker's brig boasted classic columns, wood-paneled walls, three fireplaces, milled siding, southern pine floors, and a grand second-story veranda that drank in the dramatic Sound and mountain views.

While this Southern charm oozed confederate nobility, its true nature was far from it. Maynard knew that any burgeoning metropolis needed entertainment more than pedigree, so he set about building the grandest brothel in King County, to ensure Seattle's supremacy on the Sound. Yet he also needed to cloak it in respectability to avoid incurring the wrath of Arthur Denny and the puritan set north of Yesler, so he and Felker erected a grand structure to rival Scarlet O'Hara's "Tara" and called it a boardinghouse. In order to help Felker make ends meet, Justice of the Peace Maynard even managed to arrange for the territorial government to hold court in his whorehouse (at $25 per day). At Felker House, a gentleman could of course stay the night, but most guests checked out within the hour.

Felker House was run by one of the most famous of Seattle's pioneer women, Mary Ann Conklin Boyer, who earned the nickname of "Madame Damnable" for her profane vocabulary and fiery temper. She came to Seattle after being unceremoniously dumped in Port Townsend by her husband, Captain "Bull" Conklin, and Felker took her in. Her years at sea undoubtedly taught her to stand down even the roughest of characters with her colorful language, which she could bellow in English, French, Spanish, Chinese, Portuguese, or German. The bluenose historians later euphemized her nickname to "Mother Damnable" in order to obfuscate the fact that she had diversified the hotel business with the brothel upstairs. But by any name, she was one woman not to be taken lightly. She died in 1873, and Felker House burned to the ground in the Great Fire of 1889.

## 1865–66: BROWN AND MADDOCKS SELL, CONDON MORTGAGES, TO JOHN COLLINS

In rough and tumble Seattle, the hotel business wasn't particularly lucrative—at least, it certainly wasn't for Condon et al. The partnership needed energy, capital, and, most importantly, some operational know-how. Losing confidence in the venture, Amos Brown sold his one-third interest in the venture to a John Collins (no relation to Luther) just a year later, in October 1865, while at the same time Condon granted a mortgage to Collins. Maddocks and Condon had found in Collins the energy and capital that they sorely needed, but Maddocks was resistant to turning over the management reins to Collins. Nonetheless, exactly one year later, Maddocks relented and transferred his one-third interest in the Occidental Hotel to Collins. Boren's Block One was now John Collins's problem.

{   **A SIDETRACKED BUSHWHACK**

Bertrand Collins, son of John Collins, recounted a true pioneer tale in regard to his father's purchase of Brown's interest, and the tale he told to the Seattle Times many years later bears repeating. When the time came to close the deal with Brown, an excited John Collins strapped $3,000 worth of gold around his waist in a belt. Just before heading for the mail boat that was to take him from Port Gamble to Seattle, he heard a knock at the door.

The visitor was a friendly local Indian who told him that his belt full of gold was the worst-kept secret in town and that it was reported by many "up and down the beach that he [Collins] would never reach Seattle. As soon as the Eliza Anderson was outside Foulweather Bluff, he would be killed, his body thrown overboard, and the tides would do the rest. The story would be that he got drunk and fell overboard."

Collins's native friend offered to lead him through the woods under the cover of darkness to present-day Kingston and then ferry him by canoe to Seattle. The next morning Collins arrived at the natural spring for which Spring Street in Seattle is named, his health and gold intact, thanks to the honor and loyalty of his Indian friend.

The Occidental Hotel had a new owner and a new life, but how easy it would have been to bushwhack Collins on his trip to Kingston.

The early success of the new Occidental Hotel firmly established the prominence of Boren's Block One as the heart of the city, since what precious little happened in the jewel on Elliott Bay took place there. The Fourth of July celebration, the only civic extravaganza of any significance, was held below the hotel and in adjoining Pioneer Park—our subject's "sister" wedge of pie created by the misaligning of the Maynard, Denny, and Boren plats. When presidents, celebrities, or other dignitaries came to town—President Rutherford B.

Hayes, Emma Nevada, and James Hamilton Lewis, to name three—the festivities always hit their crescendo at the Occidental. It hosted weddings and funerals, celebrations and riots, birthdays and lynchings, scholars and inebriates, all the while lodged halfway between south and north, commerce and family, sinners and saints, and Maynard and Denny.

The Occidental also lived on the waterfront, despite being two blocks west of Elliott Bay: the upland lagoon that gave shape to Maynard's Point filled at high tide directly to the south across Yesler, making the hotel's rooms with a southern exposure "waterfront" rooms at least half the day. More than a hundred years after the lagoon had been filled in, the legacy of that sometime waterfront still haunts Boren's Block One.

{ ### THE OCCIDENTAL HOTEL LAGOON

A small bit of trivia could have saved many a shark both dollars and headaches: several buildings that sit atop the former lagoon behind Maynard's Point emanate a most peculiar smell from their basements at seemingly random intervals. I spent many months and dollars trying to remedy this problem in a building I owned during the late 1990s: heating, venting, deodorizing, insulating—all, alas, to no avail.

Lo and behold, it is the ebb and flow of the briny tide as it floods around the bedrock of Maynard's Point into the hastily filled tidelands of the "Occidental Hotel lagoon" that causes this very distinctive odor. In fact, much of the land south of Yesler between Occidental Avenue and Second Avenue South shares this "historic" feature to this day.

### 1882: JOHN COLLINS INHERITS FROM CONDON

While John Condon was still legally a one-third owner of the hotel, he was not a factor in the hotel's operation after 1870, since he was busy running and living in a hotel owned by John Collins in Port Gamble. It was essentially the John Collins show at the Occidental, and Collins officially became the sole owner in 1882 upon Condon's death in Port Gamble.

Coincident with his acquisition of the last third of Boren's Block One, Collins decided that Seattle needed a renowned landmark beyond what Felker House had to offer, so he set about building a brand-new Occidental Hotel. Unlike the first incarnation, which fronted only Second Avenue, the second structure would fill the entire triangle of Boren's Block One. Collins built a four-story stucco and masonry marvel, with rows of high bay windows, ornate cast-iron moldings, and a Parisian metal mansard roof. It was magnificent, a great source of pride for Seattle's citizenry, and the crown jewel of Puget Sound.

In the sagging economic times of the mid-1880s, work was hard to find, and the unemployed masses decided to take out their frustrations on the latest round of immigrants who were driving down wages—namely, the Chinese. The Chinese riots of 1886 spared not the Occidental, since the entire staff was Chinese. An angry mob seeking to spirit away Collins's employees with murderous intent was met with the business end of a loaded shotgun, which warned that the mob might prevail but the bravest man among them would surely die. The line between courage and cowardice is a fine one, and the mob retreated. They threatened to return but never did, apparently convinced of Collins's convictions.

John Collins was indeed a man of many convictions; however, unlike Luther Collins, his were of the moral variety. He served on Seattle's first city council, helped write the first town charter, and later became mayor. He built the James Street cable car line, owned the evening newspaper the *Daily Telegraph*, and opened the Renton coal mines with partner John Leary. He partnered with Leary and Arthur Denny in forming the Leary-Collins Land Company and was one of three incorporators of the Peoples Savings Bank. He started the Seattle Gas Light Company and was an incorporator of the city's first railroad, the Seattle and Walla Walla. He died a very wealthy man, and his will probated more than 500 parcels of land in six Puget Sound counties.

Collins was an unheralded titan of Seattle, and he guided the city with a gentle, practiced hand toward many of Seattle's important firsts.

## 1889: The Great Seattle Fire

However, the events in the summer of 1889 proved more powerful than Collins's convictions, and in a single day they nearly extinguished Seattle's emergence. When the gluepot overflowed at First and Madison Street that sunny afternoon of June 6, Seattle's fire chief, Gardner Kellogg, was away attending a convention in San Francisco on modern fire suppression techniques. The flames of the Great Seattle Fire spread quickly on the northern breeze as the sparks danced from rooftop to rooftop. The outmanned and underled fire department was no match for flying embers in a wooden city.

John Collins dispatched his Chinese staff up to the roof of the Occidental with hundreds of wet blankets in hopes of calming the fiery beast; however, just like all the others doing the same, their act proved to be tantamount to firing a squirt gun at a flame-thrower. Mayor Robert Moran ordered the Colman block and other wooden structures in the fire's path dynamited in order to create a makeshift firebreak. John Collins frantically offered to buy his northerly neighbors' wooden shanties so he could do the same, but they all foolishly said no and watched their life's work burn to the ground. Collins held out hope that his masonry exterior might save the hotel, but the inferno on all sides proved too much, overcoming the hotel through its windows. By the next morning, only a pile of wreckage remained, and the complexion of every property owner in town was as ashen as the charred remains of Seattle. Boren's Block One had unloaded its constructs.

After the smoke cleared, Seattle went about the business of replacing the burned wooden structures with buildings composed of more modern fireproof materials, mostly brick and stone. A determined John Collins led the transformation and erected the third iteration of the Occidental in 1890, albeit a far more Spartan version of the former grande dame of Seattle hotels. Gone was the mansard roof and florid architecture of the second building, exchanged for the more staid and substantial Romanesque Revival style that was popular at the time, with heavy-timber post and beam construction clad in stone and masonry. It was five stories high and boasted 175 guest rooms atop five retail establishments on the ground floor (one of those establishments being the famous Sartori's, the premier purveyor of fine wines in the city). The so-called Seattle Spirit was in full swing, and unbridled optimism abounded on the Sound.

What goes up must then come down, and so did Seattle's economy in the grips of a national financial crisis during the mid-1890s. Spirit and optimism turned to panic, and Collins, weary of the fickle transient trade, converted his hotel into an office building in 1895 to stave off foreclosure. Peoples Savings Bank was encouraged to occupy the ground floor, and the upper rooms were let to any legitimate business that had a dollar for rent.

Fortunately for Collins, the multiple Alaskan gold strikes—another external event—at the end of the decade resuscitated both the city and his credit, as Seattle's population swelled with the visiting argonauts and fortune hunters. Collins decided to reenter the hotel business and converted the structure back into a hotel; however, this time he named it the Seattle Hotel, since he had relinquished the Occidental name back in 1895. Boren's Block One again had the honor of hosting the finest hotel property in the city, holding that distinction until Collins's death in 1903 when, coincidentally, the Washington Hotel opened.

{ THE DENNY HOTEL: SOON THE WASHINGTON HOTEL
Construction of the Denny Hotel began in 1889, shortly after the Great Fire, by a development group led by Arthur Denny but suffered myriad problems and interruptions in its tragically short life. The first setback experienced was the inability of the Denny-led partnership to agree on anything—specifically, which partner(s) would pay the overruns when the construction costs started to spiral out of control. Despite the build-

ing being substantially complete in 1891, the hotel was neither finished nor furnished due to the incessant squabbling of the partners. Any hope of resolution was dashed by the panic and depression of 1893, which doubled up the bolts on the shutters, since Seattle couldn't fill half the rooms it already had. The discovery in 1898 of native burial sites at the mothballed hotel brought a host of treasure hunters and grave robbers that needed neither room nor board while they defiled the grounds.

Noted developer James A. Moore subsequently bought out Denny and his former friends and finished what he renamed the Washington Hotel to great fanfare in 1903. Seattle's new premier hotel boasted superb views, an elegant Turkish smoking room, and a private tramway up Denny Hill to the Victorian luxury hotel. Teddy Roosevelt, one of its first guests, was given a typical Seattle welcome upon his arrival. As Roosevelt addressed the plebiscite from the entry lobby, a heckler, between hurling insults, loudly interrupted, "I'm a socialist, my pa was a socialist, and my grandpa was a socialist too." In an effort to quickly shut him down, the nimble president queried back, "Suppose your pa was a jackass, what would you be?" Without missing a beat, the heckler quipped, "Hell, I'd be a Republican."

Not a supporter of the massive regrading project that sought to remove the hill upon which his hotel crested, Moore refused to sell his hotel to the project and was forced to watch all the land and buildings beside him being sluiced away to Elliott Bay. The Washington Hotel sat alone and inaccessible atop its precarious perch (there is a notable photograph of this) until finally the unstoppable hoses of progress washed it away too in 1906.

## 1903: JOHN COLLINS'S WILL AND THE SEATTLE HOTEL

Competition from the Washington and other new hotels was not the only adversary the Seattle Hotel had to face. After John Collins's death in 1903, his will dictated that the Seattle Hotel was to be retained by his estate until the date his youngest daughter, Catherine, reached the legal age of eighteen—October 29, 1913. After her day of majority arrived, the six beneficiaries—his widow and five children—were free to do what they pleased with the property.

However, a hitch arose when the executors submitted their final reporting of the accounts of the estate. One of the children, Emma Collins Downey, objected. Mrs. Downey, who was Collins's daughter by a previous marriage, took issue with the executors' (one of whom was Collins's second wife, Angie) interpretation of what constituted her father's separate property, because Emma astutely recognized that she was due to receive a portion of any separate property and not a nickel of any community property.

The trouble started with some foolishness cooked up by the lawyers two weeks before John Collins's death—said foolishness being a quitclaim deed granted by Angie to John, followed shortly by a warranty deed for an undivided one-half interest granted by John to Angie. These deeds were likely executed so as to clear up any misunderstanding or confusion as to ownership of the valuable hotel, since John Collins had purchased the property in thirds over fifteen years—a period that happened to include two different wives and a nonconjugal intermission as well. The deeds said to the world that half the hotel was John's, and half was Angie's.

In 1904, the appraisers for the estate—John H. McGraw, C. D. Stimson, and John Davis—concluded that, despite the new deeds, only one-third of one-half of the Seattle Hotel was John Collins's sole and separate property, two-thirds of said half was John and Angie's community property, and the other half belonged to wife Angie as her sole and separate property. Whether this conclusion was reached in the interests of minimizing inheritance taxes or shortchanging the children is not known, but in either event, it inspired dissent. King County Superior Court heard endless angry argument about the rightful inheritance that was due the children under the will, an inheritance Mrs. Downey felt the executors had not provided. This battle would rage on for nearly twenty-five years.

In the end, though, after a bitter and bloody legal fight only a family could love, the appraisal was rebuked and the deeds were affirmed. Angie got her half and the six beneficiaries shared in the balance. True to form for Boren's Block One, the lawyers turned out to be the only winners in this one, because neither award would soon amount to much.

## 1906: TRANSFORMING THE SEATTLE HOTEL

Despite the strife from within the ownership group, wild real estate speculation due to the multiple gold strikes in Alaska in the 1890s and the inevitable arrival of the transcontinental railroad to Seattle in 1893 (after ten years in Tacoma first) marked the zenith of the Seattle Hotel's popularity, in the first decade of the twentieth century, when allegedly an offer for $1 million was received by the estate (it was valued at $180,000 in probate). The executors of the estate—Collins's widow Angie, son John Francis Collins, and friend R. L. Hodgdon—flatly refused this unprecedented price, saying arrogantly that nowhere in the city could one invest that sum and receive a return equal to the income of the Seattle Hotel.

Believing their own headlines, the divided heirs of John Collins subsequently decided to embark on an ambitious rehabilitation plan in 1906 to put an end to any question about which hotel deserved the top spot in the hierarchy of Seattle's finest lodging establishments. They immediately cleared out all the tenants of the debt-free hotel and then transformed all the rooms and ground-floor spaces—in the process erasing any evidence of its former temporary life as an office building—complete with rich mahogany paneling, coffered ceilings, and fancy glass domes. The hotel stood empty for more than a year while construction costs overran the estimates by more than $200,000, creating an overwhelming debt load from which the estate of John Collins would never recover.

In the midst of the estate's wretched excess, the inexorable northern movement of the city's center was hitting its stride, and our subject parcel of land, along with all of Pioneer Square, was fast becoming the red-headed stepchild in the Seattle family of neighborhoods, suffering municipal abuse and neglect that would continue for well over a half century. The Seattle Hotel fared no better and slowly deteriorated with the area despite the best efforts of its owners to stem the undeniable tide.

A bawdy tenderloin district that rivaled the Barbary Coast in San Francisco had grown out of the former commercial center of the city during the era of the "Lava Bed" and John Considine's box houses at the century's close, and sin and sinners were living large "below the Deadline." All respectable commerce relocated north and east. Prohibition forced the hotel's largest tenant (and also its largest debtor)—the opulent Sam Hyde's bar, the former Sartori's—into bankruptcy, and the first nail was squarely pounded in the hotel's coffin. Unfortunately, Boren's Block One sat directly on the Deadline, where creditworthy customers would never go, and no amount of lipstick on the old girl could counter three of the Seattle Hotel's curses: a bad location, location, and location.

## 1935: TRAVELERS INSURANCE COMPANY FORECLOSES

The heirs clung dearly to their father's dream and its mountain of debt until the years of the Great Depression finally dealt the fatal blow to the Collins era. In 1935, the Collins family, no longer able to make their loan payments, lost the Seattle Hotel to mortgage lender Travelers Insurance Company, which took the property back by way of a deed in lieu of foreclosure.

Even Travelers tried to spruce things up in the later half of the 1930s—more than a few building permits appear on the record—but they were all small in scale and had equal effect. Sadly, the magnificent Seattle Hotel, unable to withstand the gravity of Boren's Block One, was transformed again and relegated to be forever a flophouse, violently removed from the city's once-beating heart and dispatched to its now-throbbing groin.

CHAPTER 3:

# ISSEI

In the small seaside town of Uwajima, located on the southwest coast of Shikoku Island (seemingly light years away from Seattle and its siren's call), the finest *mikan* (tangerines) in all of Japan can be found. In the 1920s, three men from one extended family on this small Japanese island—Takemitsu Kubota, Fujimatsu Moriguchi, and Kuichi Nagai—were hatching great plans for a journey west to a new land and a new life. One of them would soon find his destiny in the rundown Seattle Hotel, but realization of his dream would, sadly, keep him awake for many nights to come.

Takemitsu was born May 24, 1902, into the Moriguchi clan in the coastal community of Kawanazu, Ehime Prefecture, but was adopted into the Kubota family shortly after birth. Since the Kubota clan had no male children to assume responsibility for the family estate—a homestead and a hillside grove of tangerines in nearby Yawatahama—they welcomed the addition of Takemitsu into their fold. Such adoptions within extended families were not an uncommon practice in rural Japan, because continuity within families was very important in traditional Japanese culture. Yet despite this proud heritage, both Kubota and Moriguchi wanted out of their agricultural bonds, and they felt America held the greatest promise for a better life.

## Leaving Japanese Farms in Search of American Gold

At the turn of the twentieth century, America's shores absorbed a tsunami of Japanese immigrants who abandoned their homeland to escape the rigid class structure of Japanese culture and carve their way to a better life. The Meiji Restoration of the late nineteenth century had infused many western ideas into Japanese culture that generated significant social and economic upheaval. Hardest hit were the peasants and farmers, who were saddled with a regressive tax burden that unwound their traditional ways of life and threatened their very survival. Industrialization was coming to Japan, and this evolution offered little to the tangerine farmer other than the opportunity to amass a family debt that would take generations to repay.

Emboldened by the Chinese Exclusion Act of 1882, which ended the influx of cheap Chinese labor to America's railroads and factories, Japan's native sons decided that they would become the next group of immigrants to fill the jobs no longer available to the Chinese. Many Japanese immigrants envisioned a five-year plan in which they would earn enough money not only to repay their family's debts but also to establish their own families upon their return to Japan. Young men from all over the island nation—many of whom were second- and third-born sons, who could not legally inherit property under Japanese law—left their homes and families seeking the port cities of Japan and a fortune in gold that they were told littered the American landscape.

First they came to Hawaii—not yet a state—to work the sugarcane fields, and then they came to the mainland. The trans-Pacific trip was no pleasure cruise: the men were stacked in "silkworm racks" in lightless ship holds, where the only source of protein they found was from their lice-infested surrounds. It was an experience not completely unlike that of the African-American diaspora. Although the Japanese immigrants were certainly free men when they were seduced into making their passage to a new life, once they were onboard the ships, their survival was wholly dependant on the profiteers who had recruited them. These pilgrims on their fortnight voyage suffered countless indignities, and many questioned the wisdom of their decision shortly after embarking. In fact, some did not survive the voyage.

Their arrival in America did little to assuage their concerns. While finding work in the sawmills, canneries, and railroads of the Pacific Northwest was relatively easy, the wages and working conditions were not. Racial exclusion, low pay, and an eighty-hour workweek were the only fortunes these ambitious immigrants encountered in coming to America. The low-hanging fruit dangling from money trees on every street corner that had been promised to them was nowhere to be found.

Dissatisfied with their lot, some of the men left these industries in the late 1890s to do what they knew best—farming—and the many fertile river valleys near the coastal cities provided plenty of land to sow. Initially, the Japanese began as laborers on farms run by their white owners, but soon the Japanese's industrious ways led them to run small farms of their own that they leased from the white landowners (since only U.S. citizens could own land). The small farms quickly became large farms as the *issei* (first-generation Japanese immigrants) began to work cooperatively and form *tanomoshi* clubs, which would lend capital and labor to member-farmers as conditions warranted. Japanese farmers began to sell their produce at Seattle's Pike Place Market in 1912, and within four years they occupied nearly three-quarters of the market's stalls. Sadly, this was just the calm before the storm.

## DISCRIMINATION EXTENDS TO NEWEST IMMIGRANTS

Just as the Chinese had discovered some twenty years before, the Asian success story was not a best seller in turn-of-the-twentieth-century Seattle—or anywhere else on the Pacific coast, for that matter. Seattle's Chinese had been rounded up en masse by a mob on a cold February night in 1886 and unceremoniously herded at gunpoint aboard a ship secured to dispatch them to San Francisco. Captain Alexander of the waiting steamer *Queen of the Pacific* refused to take them all, and roughly half were left behind on the docks in the midst of an angry throng. Violence ensued, and several men were killed in the resulting melee. President Grover Cleveland declared martial law and order was restored—however, not before Seattle's Chinese population was reduced to a few frightened individuals hiding in the town's basements, one of which was John Collins's Occidental Hotel.

Two decades later, bigotry toward the Japanese was just as evident, albeit practiced in a more subtle and codified manner by the now-prepared round eyes. The preferred weapon of discrimination now, instead of mobs with guns and ropes, was legislation, which was comprehensive and unassailable.

Congress had made "free white persons" eligible for U. S. citizenship in 1790—later amended to include African Americans after the Civil War—but Asians were not judged to be included in this category. This exclusion was made official by the U.S. Attorney in 1906.

The 1889 Washington State Constitution prohibited the sale of land to noncitizens—and again, Asians were the intended target. The distinction between citizen and noncitizen was very important, because nearly all of the opportunities and benefits accruing in American life—the right to own land, practice law, join a professional association or labor union, et cetera—were conditioned upon being an American citizen.

Cities went even further by inserting racial covenants into the plats of town additions forbidding the renting or selling of property to noncitizens, which effectively segregated the Asians from the white population in schools, churches, parks, and other hubs of social life. San Francisco took the lead in this regard, but Seattle was watching closely and mimicked the Californians' every move. (Even as late as 1960, the Japanese-American community, American-born or not, was well aware that the Lake Washington Ship Canal—the waterway that bisects Seattle east to west, from Lake Washington to Puget Sound—served as the northern boundary for any residence that was available to them. For any home they might seek north of this canal, real estate agents would not show—and sellers would not sell.)

In 1890, the Japanese population in Seattle numbered less than 200. By 1900 that sum had increased tenfold, and ten years later it had nearly tripled again. Like the Chinese before, they were an economic presence that was perceived to be making a considerable dent in the "free white person's" ability to pursue the American dream. In 1905, labor leaders and white businessmen formed the Asiatic Exclusion League at a conference in San Francisco, and a year later Bay Area Asians were completely segregated from the majority population.

Branch leagues that had been established all along the West Coast and in the industrial centers of the eastern and southwestern United States lobbied politicians for a proposed piece of national legislation called the Japanese Exclusion Act—essentially a carbon copy of the 1882 Chinese version. The mobs were poised for action. The local media, led by the *Seattle Post-Intelligencer*, conducted a propaganda campaign to illustrate the seriousness of the "yellow peril," with stories of how the Japanese were a threat to the American worker and a menace to American womanhood, warning that their acceptance would lead to a "mongrelization" of the white race.

In Vancouver, British Columbia, a group calling itself the Oriental Exclusion League staged a demonstration in 1907 in which hundreds of members marched down Powell Street ransacking the Japanese neighborhood, throwing stones, and setting fires. They repeated the attack three times and were finally repulsed by the quickly organizing Japanese, but the so-called Vancouver Riot served certain notice that the Japanese were welcome neither in Canada nor anywhere else on the West Coast.

Enough pressure was brought to bear in Washington, D.C., that President Theodore Roosevelt began negotiations with the Japanese government in 1907, which was also dissatisfied with its native sons' situation in San Francisco and elsewhere. These discussions culminated in what was known as the "Gentleman's Agreement," whereby Japan would agree to immediately stop exporting its unemployed masses to the United States if the Americans would agree to be more polite hosts and permit limited immigration of *issei* wives, children, and family members. (The immigration loophole for wives of the transplants created a whole new wave of Japanese immigrants, which were distinctly feminine, the so-called "picture brides" married to men in America upon whom they had never laid eyes.)

Unfortunately, the limitations contained in the Gentleman's Agreement did not satisfy the fearmongers. In 1913 California passed the Alien Land Law prohibiting ownership of land by noncitizens (read: Asians).

Five years later, Seattle businessmen formed the Anti-Japanese League, which accused the Japanese of stealing the jobs that were vacated by white American youth who had been called to the front lines to fight in World War I. The league, in cooperation with the American Legion, coordinated their racist lobbying efforts to ensure that Japanese workers lost their jobs to the returning servicemen, despite the fact that more than 700 *issei* men had also enlisted to heed President Woodrow Wilson's call to "save the world for democracy."

In 1920, the Seattle City Council enacted an ordinance prohibiting the issuance of a business license to any noncitizen. In 1921, Washington adopted its own Alien Land Law—similar to the California legislation—which continued the legitimization of bigotry against Asians in an open and notorious fashion.

The pressure continued to build until finally Congress reneged on the Gentleman's Agreement and passed the Immigration Act of 1924, which was intended to permanently put an end to any and all Asian immigration. Native Americans, evacuated to reservations many years before, were probably wondering what took the white man so long.

{ TAKUJI YAMASHITA: ONE MAN'S EXPERIENCE
The never-ending trials of one Japanese man, Takuji Yamashita, speak volumes to the exclusion and challenges faced by Japanese immigrants coming to America. Yamashita, who left his hometown on Shikoku Island in the late 1890s, got his first

job in a new land with the help of Kyuhachi Nishii, who, like Yamashita, also hailed from Ehime-ken (Ehime Prefecture). Nishii owned a restaurant in Tacoma and had helped more than fifty other new arrivals from his region find jobs upon their arrival on American soil.

Once settled, in 1900 Yamashita then enrolled in the University of Washington law school, which had been founded by John T. Condon (coincidentally, the son of the Occidental Hotel founder of the same name) just one year before. Condon also enrolled in his first classes women and Jews. After graduating and passing his bar exam in 1902, Yamashita was denied the right to practice law because he was Asian born, despite having been given his naturalization papers four days before graduation.

Bigotry and exclusion had now been codified into Washington State law regarding the qualifications for practicing law—by application of the citizenship condition. Yamashita represented himself in his fight to gain the right to join the bar (as well as become a citizen), which he eventually lost in the Washington State Supreme Court because the U.S. Congress had not allowed Asians to become citizens.

In 1922, Yamashita next attempted to gain the right to own real property. As noncitizens, Asians could not own land individually because of Washington State's Alien Land Law passed in 1921, so Yamashita and an associate tried to form a Washington corporation for the purpose of holding land. When the Secretary of State denied the application, Yamashita sued. He lost his case in both the lower court and the Washington State Supreme Court, again. He appealed to the U.S. Supreme Court, which agreed to hear the case—albeit bundled with the suits of two other Japanese men who were also suing to retain naturalization rights (which had been granted to them as war veterans). In all cases, the lower court's rulings were affirmed.

Weary from his legal battles, Yamashita moved to the Kitsap Peninsula and operated a strawberry farm and a pair of hotels in Bremerton and Silverdale, only to lose them when he and more than 100,000 Japanese were shipped to internment camps during World War II. He spent the rest of his American life as a houseboy in Seattle before he moved back to Japan in 1957. He died two years later in the place of his birth, Yawatahama (the same small town on Shikoku Island from which the Kubota clan hailed).

It was not all bad news for Yamashita, since he did finally live to see veterans' naturalization rights affirmed in 1935 and citizenship rights granted to Japanese in 1952. He did not, however, outlive the bigotry he fought so hard to reverse, and he never witnessed Washington voters finally repealing the Alien Land Law in 1966—after the fourth try—nor was he alive later when in 1973 aliens were given the right to practice law. The Washington State Supreme Court posthumously inducted Yamashita as an honorary member of the bar in 2001 in an attempt to right the wrongs of nearly a century before. A dozen descendants of Yamashita (as well as Washington's Chinese-American Governor Gary Locke) proudly looked on.

## TAKEMITSU KUBOTA ARRIVES IN SEATTLE

The mighty struggles of Japanese immigrants such as Takuji Yamashita were no doubt well circulated back home in Ehime-ken; however, Takemitsu Kubota was not deterred. Married with three children in Japan by the age of 21, Kubota nonetheless planned his migration overseas despite the hardships he must have anticipated. He is once quoted as saying he reached Seattle's shores in 1923 (one year before the Immigration Act was passed) and he once testified in a trial deposition that he arrived in Seattle in January 1926. However, there is no public record or other evidence of Kubota in Seattle or Tacoma until 1930. Kubota's cousin, Fujimatsu Moriguchi, first appears in the public record as a driver for Seattle's Main Fish Company in 1928, but Kubota is first recorded in Seattle two years later in 1930. Exactly when Kubota entered the country—as either a legal or illegal immigrant—only he knows for sure, but what is known is that his cousin Moriguchi was smuggled into Seattle just prior to Kubota's arrival.

Like most of their fellow countrymen from Ehime Prefecture, both Kubota and Moriguchi went to Tacoma initially to enlist the help of Japanese pioneer and restaurateur Kyuhachi Nishii, one of the first Japanese in the Puget Sound region, to get their start in America. The Grand Café in Tacoma provided Kubota his first employment in America, as a dishwasher and a cook.

After several months, the long hours and very low wages of restaurant work persuaded Kubota to change direction and try his luck in a sawmill, but he left after only two weeks because, as Kubota himself explained, "I wasn't strongly built and couldn't work rhythmically enough to sort the floating logs." So he went to Great Falls, Montana, in 1928 to work for the Great Northern Railway at the request of his family in order to find his uncle, Shikanosuke Nagai. Nagai was supposed to be sending money back home periodically to Japan from his work on the railroad gangs, but for some reason not even a letter had found its way back to Ehime-ken. Kubota went to find out why.

After the long journey overland, Kubota found Nagai alive and well in Montana, albeit with a bad gambling habit that seemed to separate him from his wages as soon as he earned them. Not wanting to fall in with the gambling crowd, Kubota decided to avoid trouble and took a job in the roundhouse washing steam engines and cleaning wheels.

When Kubota went to work for the railroad in 1928, Fujimatsu Moriguchi, who had been driving for the Main Fish Company in Seattle, opened an Asian food store at 1512 Broadway in Tacoma, where he made a Japanese fish cake, *kamaboko*, that he sold to local Japanese fishermen and sawmill workers. Moriguchi, along with his brother Saisuke, named the store after the city where he learned his trade— Uwajima on Shikoku—and called it Uwajimaya (-*ya* means "store"). The business remained in Tacoma until the family was sent away to the internment camps in 1942 pursuant to President Franklin Roosevelt's Executive Order 9066. After World War II ended, they relocated to Seattle to rejoin family and friends and opened a new Uwajimaya at 422 South Main Street in *Nihonmachi* (Japan-town), within the original donation claim of Doc Maynard.

After two years of hot, dirty work in Montana building a nest egg for his family, Kubota returned to Seattle, where he called for his wife (who was still in Japan) to join him in his grand adventure. Since 1924 and the passage of the Immigration Act had come and gone, how she got here is unknown. Unfortunately, shortly after arriving in America, his wife, Misano, died, leaving the two surviving children, Ichiro and Misako, behind in Yawatahama with relatives—and Kubota alone again in his new homeland.

Within a few years of his wife's passing, Takemitsu Kubota—who now added the anglicized Henry to his name, to become Henry T. Kubota, or H. T. to his associates—was introduced to a woman named Easter Yoshiko, a North Dakota native who was *kibei*, that is, born in America but schooled in Japan. She returned to America after her education and made her living as a live-in helper to families of naval officers in Bremerton, from whom she learned western etiquette and cooking. Easter and H. T. were married shortly after their introduction and thereafter began their long life together in Seattle, raising three children and operating a series of small hotels south of the Deadline.

## ISSEI, NISEI, AND KIBEI

The marriage of H. T. to Easter was most unusual in that it represented a union of a first-generation immigrant—*issei*—and a second-generation—*nisei*—woman. While the distinction between generations may seem trivial to non-Japanese-Americans, the cultural differences between Japanese immigrants and their children was significant—more so than the normal generational gap—due to a number of conspiring elements.

For starters, the *issei* arrived on American soil during a relatively short period of time—that is, a twenty-five-year period around the turn of the twentieth century—before the spigot was slowed by President Theodore Roosevelt with the Gentlemen's Agreement in 1907 and completely shut off by Congress with the Immigration Act of 1924. This effectively limited the age group of the *issei*, who were for all intents stuck in a time warp, condemned to swim in a cultural pond that was not to be restocked for nearly half a century.

Added to this gap was the wide cultural and language disparity between the generations. The *issei* were socialized in the highly ordered and disciplined Japanese society, in which ceremony, obligation, and status played significant roles. They bowed gracefully from the waist to greet their fellow *issei*, spoke only Japanese with its subtle modulation, and formed close associations according to their native *ken* (prefectures).

Conversely, the *nisei* didn't want to be a "hyphenated American"; they were Yankees through and through. They were born into the wild and chaotic west, where lawlessness and rugged independence guided the course of events. They had anglicized names such as Henry and Easter, spoke colloquial English, knew little of Japanese custom and tradition, and were fed a steady diet of American popular culture.

While some might say this set of facts is really no different from what any other immigrant group experienced, the important differences lie in two particulars: the disparity of the merging cultures—the vast majority of American immigrants were occidental, not oriental—and the abrupt damming of the flow of new Japanese immigrants by federal law.

Thus, not only would compatibility be an issue to an *issei-nisei* union, but it also was rare that they would be near the same age, owing to this narrow window of original Japanese immigration. In what surely was important to H. T., Easter was *kibei*, which gave her the grace to move adroitly through both the Japanese and the Japanese-American worlds.

The *kibei* represented an interesting third class of individuals within the subculture of Japanese life in America, because they were *nisei* and of *nisei* age but had *issei* values. These *nisei* were sent to Japan for their education and socialization because staying in America was never part of their parents' plan. The *kibei* subscribed to, among other things, traditional Japanese gender archetypes, but the *issei* men were typically far too old for the *kibei* women, and the *nisei* women had no interest in playing the role of docile and subservient wife to the *kibei* men.

Thus, the *kibei* were living in a lonely world in which they were shunned by the only two subcultures that would claim them. Had Japanese immigration to America been permitted to continue past 1924 (one reason the *issei* sent their children to be schooled and socialized in Japan in the first place), there would have been no need to identify *kibei* as such, because new *issei* would be arriving every day. The *kibei* would have melded nicely into the second wave of *issei* immigrants, but since there weren't any, the *kibei* were isolated within their own community. Luckily for Easter, she was an older *nisei* who happened to find a young *issei*, while at the same time she possessed an attribute no *issei* man thought he could never enjoy: American citizenship.

## H. T. KUBOTA AND CHARLES CLISE

In 1930, upon his return to Seattle from Montana, Kubota found employment working for the Grand Union Laundry Company, which undoubtedly led him to what would be the focus of his life's work: hospitality. He got his first opportunity managing a hotel in 1931, the New Home Hotel on Dearborn Street, where he did everything from making beds to cleaning toilets. He next managed the nearby Crown Hotel in 1932, the Rawling Hotel in 1934, the Cherry Hotel in 1937, the Arlington Hotel in 1939, and the Loring Hotel in 1940. With the exception of the Arlington Hotel, all the hotels Kubota managed were small.

Kubota often managed two hotels at a time without a single employee, which, during the Depression years, was the only way to survive. Sleep was a luxury for the guests only. It was hard and unglamorous work, but in time it provided him a standard of living that surpassed most of his *issei* countryman—a point of considerable import to H. T. He became one of the so-called "Big Three" in the Japanese Hotel Operators' Association—a well-deserved honor—

and humbly assumed a leadership role among his peers from his native prefecture as well as within the greater Japanese-American community. He also gained the notice of a man who would prove a providential partner during the war years.

Henry Kubota met Charles Clise in 1938 as a result of a transaction involving the Arlington Hotel. Clise was president of Arlington Hotel, Inc., which he had formed with two associates (R. Kline Hillman and S. J. Mullally) for the purpose of purchasing the Arlington Hotel at 1019 First Avenue. Clise was not much interested in running hotels, so he assigned that task to Henry Kubota, whom Clise selected due to his record for managing hotels whose prime had long past.

Charles Clise was a member of a prominent Seattle family that had extensive real estate holdings downtown. The eldest son of family patriarch J. W. Clise, Charles made his fortune and reputation by purchasing an astonishing portfolio of land in an area known as the Regrade, in the north end of downtown Seattle—most for only the price of the unpaid taxes on the land in the aftermath of the Great Depression. He was a shrewd and clever operator who was not best known for his charitable ways.

The first Clise in Seattle, J. W., had the classic pioneer mix of strong work ethic and indefatigable will. After coming west with his Mennonite bride, Anna Herr Clise, J. W. first settled shortly before the Great Seattle Fire at Ebey's Landing on Whidbey Island with intent to farm. Barley, wheat, and rye were to be his principal crops, which he decided he would barge to Seattle in order to receive the most favorable prices. The next autumn, after landing in a stormy and windswept Seattle, he hired a man to watch his barge while he set out to complete the sale of his first crop. In his brief absence, the frothy seas of Elliott Bay tipped the barge, and his crop was swept into the water and away with the tide. Penniless and embittered by the hired man's failure to protect the fruit of his year's labor, he immediately sold his farm and moved to Seattle the day after the Seattle fire—June 7, 1889. That day began the making of the Clise family empire, which has thrived throughout the myriad fortunes and misfortunes of the Seattle real estate market with a combination of toughness and sound business practices, notably a decided aversion to debt.

Ironically, it was J. W. Clise who, upon making the acquaintance of typewriter magnate L. C. Smith, sold him eight Pioneer Square properties sight unseen in 1890, including the Smith Tower site. J. W. Clise was also one of the famous Tlingit totem pole thieves, the so-called Committee of Fifteen who delivered the stolen totem to Pioneer Place Park—adjacent to Boren's Block One and the opposite triangle that was created by the misaligning of the Maynard, Boren, and Denny plats—to great fanfare and acclaim in October 1890. Some time later, eight of the offending fifteen, including Clise, were indicted by the state of Alaska for the alleged theft; however, the charges were dismissed after a newly appointed federal judge for the district of Alaska was entertained at the Rainier Club in Seattle. J. W. Clise recalled many years later that "the entertainment was such a remarkable success that upon his taking his judicial position in Alaska, one of his first acts was to dismiss the suit."

{ **J. W. Clise: Gentleman Farmer**
In 1904, Clise purchased a sizable parcel of land located along the banks of the Sammamish Slough and transformed it into an estate he called Willowmoor (in 1962, it became King County's first park, Marymoor Park). What had begun as a hunting lodge became a world-renowned farm, where Clise exercised his considerable passion for the agricultural arts. Notably, he bred Scottish Ayrshire cattle there, which attracted international attention. Automobile tycoon Henry Ford insisted that the only milk served at his table would be from Willowmoor Ayrshires. Also suitably impressed, the Japanese government sent a trade delegation to stay at Willowmoor in 1914 to learn about Clise's farming techniques. Forty Japanese dairymen spent several days at the farm, where the Clise children, including Charles, likely got their first exposure to Japanese people and culture. Henry Kubota may have been the primary beneficiary of that exposure.

His son Charles Clise's purchases in the post-Depression era were mostly land plays—the idea being to wait out the bad times and sell into the good times. Charles was not overly concerned with the current tenants or the current income, but he paid close attention to the purchase price and the property location. Charles Clise and Henry Kubota made a good team: Clise leased and managed the Arlington Hotel's retail levels to mostly white business owners, and Kubota rented the ninety-six flophouse rooms to transient workmen and bachelors.

Clise was very pleased with Kubota's performance, but more importantly, he was impressed by Kubota's willingness to keep his property commitments despite the turbulence brought by the coming war.

## KUBOTA AND THE SEATTLE HOTEL

By 1941, Kubota had unloaded most of his hotel management contracts, which laid the groundwork for his most ambitious plan to date. The mother of all Seattle flophouses, the Seattle Hotel, was the biggest and most influential hotel property in the rundown fleabag category, owing to the fact that it had a storied past, sat next to the most important landmark in the city—the Smith Tower—and was located in what Kubota called the "Seattle District" (as opposed to *Nihonmachi*). Travelers Insurance Company, which had foreclosed on the property in 1935, had horribly mismanaged the once-premier hotel, and the absentee ownership had helped neither the hotel's condition nor its income statement. So Kubota decided to make a run at the old girl.

In February 1941, H. T. enlisted the assistance of three ambitious *nisei*—William Mimbu, Paul Yoshio Tomita, and Frank Kinomoto—to help him perform a task that he himself by law was unable to do—that is, to form a Washington State corporation. Being of majority age and, most importantly, citizens of the United States, the three *nisei* filed the original articles of incorporation for the Seattle Hotel Building Corporation (SHBC) on February 11, 1941, and in the process each subscribed to purchase one share of the corporation stock—out of an aggregate 120 shares. Shortly thereafter, the corporation made a perfunctory filing to satisfy the state's never-ending thirst for information, and a new name suddenly appeared prominently among the baby-faced *nisei*: H. T. Kubota. The three *nisei* incorporators had each put in the first $100 of the $12,000 initial capitalization, but Kubota was the man.

{ CORPORATE TRIVIA

Within the original SHBC articles of incorporation is Article VII, which provided that "shares of this corporation may be issued for such consideration in labor ..."—the inference being that stock ownership of the entity could be transferred to others (read: *issei*) through the application of elbow grease as time went by. State law required that majority ownership of a corporation be vested in citizens, especially a corporation that intended to own real property, hence the three American-born incorporators were a necessary condition to fulfill this requirement; however, the obfuscated purpose of Article VII (and the corporation itself) was to circumvent Washington State's 1921 Alien Land Law and provide for the inevitable transfer of real property to an alien.

At the first meeting of the SHBC's board of directors, on February 15, 1941, a resolution was unanimously adopted authorizing the corporation to purchase the Seattle Hotel and all of Boren's Block One for $100,000, in accordance with the terms and conditions of a real estate contract that was an attachment to the resolution. At the second meeting of the board of directors, Henry T. Kubota was elected its president.

According to the corporation's stock subscription agreement, Kubota held only a minority interest in the SHBC, but that was just for the benefit of the law. In reality, it mattered little who owned the stock because the corporation wasn't really running the show—it just held title. Soon after the purchase of the hotel, SHBC entered into a lease with Henry T. Kubota, who was hired to manage the property. The rent due under the lease was scheduled to roughly match the payments due under the real estate contract, so it was financially a wash for the SHBC. The deal was structured so that the operator, who was responsible for the profit of the investment, got the benefit of his industry—and that man was Henry Takemitsu Kubota.

It was a good arrangement for all concerned. Kubota controlled enough of the SHBC through his extended family to prevent any corporate actions that were detrimental to his interests, while at the same time the corporation was a vehicle through which he could both own real property and borrow the funds he needed to buy it. No longer would he have to dwell in the shadows of American business. He could openly run his businesses without the fear of being exposed as an alien or be taken advantage of by unscrupulous white landlords. And the young *nisei* got to learn a thing or two from the master himself while opening a few doors and earning a few dollars along the way. Everybody was happy.

On December 4, 1941—three days before the Japanese would attack Pearl Harbor—the SHBC board of directors held a special meeting to discuss a proposed purchase of the Cherry Hotel, the terms of which Kubota had been negotiating for several months. H. T. had been managing the hotel since 1937, but now he had the means—in the SHBC—by which to truly profit from the fruit of his labors. The board approved entering into the real estate contract to buy the property for the sum of $40,500, and a second hotel was in the portfolio of the SHBC. It was a proud day for Kubota, because he was finally able to close his eyes and dream the sweet American dream.

## 1942: EXECUTIVE ORDER 9066

Unfortunately, as has so often been the case in and around Boren's Block One, Kubota's good fortune was about to change. The Japanese made good on their promise to Hitler and attacked Pearl Harbor, engaging the Americans in the Pacific to distract them from the European theater of World War II. In an instant, the gravity of the situation turned Kubota's world upside down.

In the early morning hours of December 8, 1941, the FBI rounded up several Japanese men who were suspected of being potential spies, ripping them from their beds and their families for interrogation. The *nikkei*—persons of Japanese decent—on American soil were thrown into a state of shock and chaos; the frowns to which they had become accustomed turned to angry scowls and howls of "damn Jap!" The various anti-Japanese organizations pointed to the attack in the Pacific and demanded government action to rid America once and for all of the "yellow peril." The word was out that trouble was coming, and any *nikkei* who could leave the West Coast—students and/or those with family inland—did so, packing their bags and heading east.

Initially, the Japanese-American community believed that only *issei* would be subject to incarceration, since they were technically Japanese nationals. Surely the U. S. Constitution would protect innocent American-born citizens (*nisei*) from illegal incarceration—or so thought the *nisei* sons and daughters, who began to learn the inner workings of their fathers' businesses in anticipation of managing them in their parents' absence. "Someone will intervene—they must," they thought. But no one did.

On February 19, 1942, shock gave way to fear as President Roosevelt signed Executive Order 9066, which authorized the relocation of "any and all persons from designated military zones." The phrase "any and all persons" meant anybody with a trace of Japanese blood, and the *nisei* now realized that their parents would have plenty of company in their relocation. The War Relocation Authority was created, and the West Coast was divided into 108 exclusion zones. Sites were determined for "assembly centers," and the Japanese community braced for the worst. A strict curfew was placed on the Japanese community that restricted them to their homes from 8:00 p.m. to 6:00 a.m.

On March 30, 1942, a couple hundred Japanese from Bainbridge Island, *issei* and *nisei* alike, became the first community in Washington State to be evacuated, after being given a one-week

notice to settle their affairs. The order for the 7,000 members of
Seattle's Japanese community to report to the assembly center at
the Puyallup fairgrounds came on April 21, where all individuals
of Japanese descent were to be catalogued and removed from the
Pacific coast to relocation camps throughout the American interior.
H. T. Kubota's dream had become a nightmare.

"Be it remembered, that on the 21st day of March, 1942 ... there
was called a special meeting of the directors of the Seattle Hotel
Building Corporation," began the entry in the corporation's minutes
book. Discussion centered on "the proposed evacuation of Japanese
from the Seattle District, and it was decided that the Seattle and
Cherry Hotel properties owned by the corporation could be best
managed by entering into a property management agreement with
Chas. F. Clise, Agent, Inc." The agreement was signed the same day.
A later entry listed a motion duly made, seconded, and unanimously
carried: "Resolved, that H. T. Kubota be, and he is hereby appointed
as, manager of said corporation with full power to act on its behalf
in every respect." Meetings would surely be impossible for an indefinite amount of time, so each director signed a general power of
attorney in favor of Kubota.

Clise agreed to manage the ground floor and basement tenants of
the Seattle Hotel for Kubota during the war in return for 5 percent
of the gross rents, since the retail shop rents were apparently sufficient to make the $700 monthly payment due to Travelers Insur-
ance Company. Many hotel rooms were left vacant in wartime, since
most of the customers were overseas fighting (although Kubota
did keep the hotel running to some degree in the hands of a loyal
white tenant—H. L. Beagle—as some other Japanese hoteliers did).
Clise's accommodation to Kubota was no small gift: if Clise failed
to make the payments under Kubota's real estate contract to Travelers, Kubota's down payment of $12,000 would surely be lost. Clise
also took care of the Cherry Hotel and Kubota's personal residence
during the war.

## INTERNMENT AND ENLISTMENT

In May 1942, the Kubota family—H. T. and Easter and their three children, Doris, Thomas, and newborn Irene—was detained within the barbed wire of Camp Harmony—yes, Camp Harmony—at the present-day Western Washington Fairgrounds in Puyallup, Washington. All their earthly possessions were locked away in the Seattle Hotel, save the few they carried in their hands.

The past few months had been the most stressful of their lives as they put their affairs in order and prepared to face an indefinite internment in an unknown location. Camp Harmony was an intermediate stop, but where would they end up? What to pack? What would be needed? And for how long?

After scurrying around in a panic to ready themselves before being driven from their homes for an uncertain future, the pause that was their lot at Camp Harmony must have been quite a shock. Since his arrival in the United States, Henry Kubota's long days had been filled with the labors of his livelihood, and he had never had a moment's rest, let alone a week off. Now he was trapped in an 18-foot-by-20-foot room with absolutely nothing to do but anticipate the loss of everything he had worked for. The change must have been staggering.

Later, Kubota and his family were shipped to Camp Minidoka in Idaho, from where Charles Clise was instrumental in securing Kubota's release, writing a letter in support of Kubota's "parole" to work at a Colorado beet farm in 1942. Clise wrote that his client demonstrated "ability and competency of outstanding quality" and that "there have been many occasions when, had he so desired, he might have taken advantage of conditions to avoid his obligations, but in every instance I have found his integrity to have been outstanding and without limitation of any sort. He is a man of great character and I am hopeful that he can be granted every privilege properly due to him under the circumstances." Kubota was permitted to relocate—with his family—from Minidoka to Denver, Colorado, on November 16, 1942.

The next shareholders meeting of the SHBC occurred in Denver on March 25, 1943, wherein, remarkably, all but one of the directors was recorded as present. "Due to the evacuation and volunteering of the stockholders into the armed forces of the United States of America, the stockholders will be unable to hold any future meeting; we hereby waive all the statutory and by-law requirements of said corporation." The *nisei* that made up the stockholder list had all enlisted in the highly decorated 442nd Regimental Combat Team, whose motto was, ironically, "Go for broke!"

The 442nd served in the European theater during seven major campaigns from 1943 to 1945, wherein they distinguished themselves as "some of the best goddamn fighters in the U. S. Army," according to Lieutenant Mark Clark, commander of the Fifth Army. The unit received one Congressional Medal of Honor, seven Presidential Unit Citations, 18,000 individual decorations, and nearly 10,000 casualties. Enlistees from Minidoka suffered the highest number of injured and dead, but, remarkably, all the *nisei* stockholders of the SHBC came home.

## RETURNING TO POSTWAR SEATTLE

The end of the war and the return of the Japanese to their former homes was not exactly a ticker-tape parade. Many returned to vandalized homes or no homes at all. Businesses that had once thrived were in ruins or gone. White employers were not exactly rolling out the welcome mat for the unemployed veterans of the 442nd (or any other Japanese, for that matter); signs read "no Japs wanted." Many *issei* and *nisei* had lost friends and relatives in the atomic bombings of Hiroshima and Nagasaki. It was a difficult time for the *nikkei*, to say the least.

Henry Takemitsu Kubota, however, was not deterred. At the cessation of hostilities, upon Kubota's return to Seattle in 1946, Clise turned the Seattle Hotel, the Cherry Hotel, and Kubota's personal residence back over to Kubota, for which he earned the Japanese family's deep gratitude and respect. Letters from Clise to

Kubota during the war described, among other things, the difficulty Clise had managing the affairs of a principal with whom he could not communicate in a timely fashion. Clise was forced to juggle monies—without authorization from Kubota—between the three properties in order to meet obligations as they arose (many of which were not normal or recurring). Drastic times called for drastic measures and Clise put his own agency at risk in an effort to keep H. T.'s businesses above water. One sweet letter from Clise to Kubota detailed the Christmas gifts Kubota (a Buddhist) had provided to the employees of both the hotel and the Clise Agency in appreciation of their efforts while he was interned in Minidoka, as well as a gift of Christmas poinsettias to Clise. Grateful indeed, for most Japanese businessmen were not so fortunate to have a man like Charles Clise on their side.

Kubota's first task once he was back in Seattle was to shore up his empire, which had weighed heavily on his mind for the seemingly endless days of his internment. He paid off the contract due Travelers Insurance Company for the Seattle Hotel by refinancing the debt, and on July 31, 1946, the SHBC finally received the deed to Boren's Block One (on a real estate conditional sales contract, title does not pass until the contract is fulfilled). With the title now in hand, he would no longer fear losing his prized asset, which he had come perilously close to losing during the war.

He next bought the Arlington Hotel from Charles Clise. Then, as he had done with the Seattle Hotel, he master-leased the Cherry Hotel for $350 per month and purchased the furniture and fixtures for $4,000 from the SHBC. A year later, the Cherry Hotel furniture was resold to the SHBC for $8,000 and the entire property sold to a man named Chang Hei Lee (since the Chinese were viewed as allies during the war, the American government wanted to keep sentiments between the two countries high, so the Chinese Exclusion Act had been repealed). The manipulation of sums paid for leases, combined with personal property transfers between Kubota and the SHBC, became the principal mechanism of the SHBC for transferring wealth to the person creating it. Kubota was again free to pursue his dream; the foundation of his empire was back on solid ground, thanks in large part to the able assistance of *nisei* lawyer William Mimbu.

William Y. Mimbu had a considerable following within the Japanese community. Born in Seattle, he had graduated from University of Washington law school and married Merry Masuda, sister of prominent *nisei* attorney Thomas Shinao Masuda. When the war broke out, Mimbu had been assigned the position of block captain "A" at Camp Harmony in Puyallup, which earned him the attention of the camp commanders. The *nisei* had quickly organized a government at the camp, with a mayor, a newspaper, street names, et cetera—to create order out of chaos, and had elected Mimbu mayor. Soon identified as one of four suspected troublemakers at the camp—along with Kenji Okeda, S. Hosokowa, and fellow SHBC shareholder Frank Kinomoto—Mimbu had been shipped off to Stockton, California, and later to a camp in Arkansas called McGehee, where "dangerous types" were sequestered far from the Pacific coast. In 1944 Mimbu had been released from McGehee to work in Wisconsin.

Mimbu, for most of his adult life, had been Henry Kubota's attorney, and the relationship had served both men well. Kubota's job was to go out and make his mark in the Seattle real estate community, and Mimbu's task was to make sure his client did not run afoul of the law—the Alien Land Law and others. The corporate records of the SHBC are as officious and tidy as any that one would ever see: not a single misspelling, with every "i" dotted and each "t" crossed. Mimbu had cooked up a host of schemes over the years for Kubota—establishing sister corporations to the SHBC, installing proprietorships to channel income, using stock purchases instead of fee interests to buy real property—and did a most credible job protecting his client.

Unfortunately, despite the two men's business savvy, Kubota's luck did not improve. The Seattle Hotel had, like many of the unreinforced masonry structures of Pioneer Square, suffered extensive damage in the magnitude 7.2 earthquake of 1949, and Kubota rightly questioned its ability to withstand another. SHBC borrowed $60,000 for repairs to the sagging structure, but this sum proved inadequate. The elevators also needed extensive renovation, and $14,000 more was needed to get them running again. Kubota brought the old girl back with these capital infusions, but she was no longer the shining jewel of yesteryear, and the many years of neglect from the previous owners (Travelers Insurance Company and the estate of John Collins) were showing. After all he had endured, Kubota must have wondered, "What else can go wrong?" Had anyone told him, he wouldn't have liked the answer.

CHAPTER 4:

# EVOLUTION

Japanese immigrant Henry T. Kubota had formed the Seattle Hotel Building Corporation and purchased Boren's Block One from Travelers Insurance Company for $100,000 by way of a conditional sales contract in February 1941. But his former countrymen in Japan having bombed Pearl Harbor perched Kubota on a very slippery slope. President Roosevelt's subsequent Executive Order 9066 authorizing the evacuation of all Japanese to the internment camps crushed Kubota's dream of running the Seattle Hotel. When he finally returned to Seattle after the war, he regained the hotel, only to soon find it needing extensive repairs from a powerful earthquake. He needed some good news.

He didn't get any.

Kubota was also subjected to continual harassment by the city of Seattle and King County—the latter commencing legal action in 1952 to abate the Seattle Hotel as a public nuisance and fine SHBC and Kubota for aiding and abetting certain alleged acts of prostitution. The stakes for Kubota were incredibly high, for if found guilty, he faced deportation since he was not an American citizen. Of course, many illegal acts unacceptable to the bluenose set were going on south of the Deadline (Yesler Way), but it had been that way for more than fifty years. It was the Skid Road, after all, and the troubled Boren's Block One sat squarely at ground zero.

The trial court, recognizing this fact, as well as Kubota's personal integrity, held that the hotel was not a nuisance and that the defendants did not aid or abet prostitution or any other acts of lewdness.

King County Prosecutor Charles O. Carroll ignored the dismissal of his charges by the lower court and appealed the decision directly to the Supreme Court of Washington, which quickly affirmed the trial court decision in its entirety, adding that Carroll's "attack ... was without merit." No new evidence was presented at a second trial other than the prosecutor's fiery will and endless legal resources, but a message was sent nonetheless: if you want to do business in my town, you play by my rules.

{ CHARLES CARROLL: CORRUPTION SCANDAL

Charles Carroll—former University of Washington football star, the man who indicted Teamster boss Dave Beck for grand larceny, and Seattle's incarnation of J. Edgar Hoover—saw his political career come to an abrupt end not long after the 1952 legal action again Kubota, when he was indicted for being at the center of a police corruption scandal. State and local laws had restricted liquor sales, gambling, and other vices, but these laws were selectively enforced south of the Deadline. Businessmen had two choices: they could either pay protection money to the police or face the wrath of Charlie "Fair Catch" Carroll (critics accused him of never taking risks).

When the dust had settled, the law enforcement community, from top to bottom—beat cops, vice detectives, and officials at City Hall—were all found to have had their hand in the cookie jar, taking bribes from businesses that wanted cops to look the other way. Charlie "Fair Catch" was forced to resign.

Kubota's only mistake had been refusing to be one of Carroll's shakedown victims. That, and clinging stubbornly to Boren's Block One.

## 1960: KUBOTA LEASES BOREN'S BLOCK ONE TO THE BRUCE SECOND AND JAMES CORPORATION

So in 1959, when Kubota was approached by a group calling itself the Bruce Second and James Corporation that said they were interested in building a six-story office building atop a parking garage on his land, it should come as no bombshell that he listened very carefully. Two dreary decades of cleaning hotel rooms, internment, recovering from earthquakes, and withstanding malicious prosecution had, for Kubota, dulled the luster of the Seattle Hotel considerably. Finally, when they mentioned that Standard Oil of California, an American institution with an international reputation, was to be the primary tenant of the building, Kubota's mind was made up. He would ground lease Boren's Block One and the terminally ill Seattle Hotel.

A few months later, on March 24, 1960, SHBC—represented by its corporate secretary, attorney William Y. Mimbu—and the Bruce Second and James Corporation entered into a ground lease, which would expire in forty years and included a pair of ten-year extension options. Based on the Bruce Second and James Corporation people's stated intent, this seemed an attractive arrangement to Kubota, mostly due to the lease's estate tax planning advantages (President Franklin Roosevelt had increased the top marginal rate for estate tax to 70 percent in 1935), as well as its ability to help him avoid capital gains tax (since it was not a sale).

Under the lease, SHBC was to receive a nominal ground rent of $1,500 a month for thirty years (the rent for years thirty-one through forty would be increased to $1,725 per month), after which time the Kubota heirs—he correctly predicted he would not survive the lease term—would either be the proud new owner of a valuable six-story office building, in the best case, or, in the worst, get to increase the rent to a market rate for the pair of ten-year extension options before becoming the proud new owner of the office building.

Given Kubota's long-term investment philosophy, it was a fine plan. Kubota was converting taxable annual income into capital appreciation that wouldn't be recognized until after his death—and it just might have worked, except for the presence of a small piece of trivia: under the lease, he had no control over what the Bruce Second and James Corporation could do with his land.

## AN UNFORTUNATE LEASE

In the esoteric world of ground leases, Kubota's document was a nightmare, from the landlord's perspective. On every point of legitimate concern to a ground lessor, the lease was either silent or decidedly favoring the ground lessee. On the major issues—such as rent, lender subordination, or control over what could be built on the land—he gave away the store in anticipation of future benefits. On those points that were very technical in nature and/or guided the parties in the occurrence of some unlikely event—such as condemnation—the lease was a case study in prudent tenant representation. In fairness, Kubota had no previous experience with this type of transaction and, from the looks of it, neither had Mimbu. But one thing is certain, though: Kubota should never have signed that lease, because within a matter of months all those mistakes would weigh on him like a ton of concrete.

To Kubota's utter chagrin, the Bruce Second and James Corporation never did construct that handsome six-story office building for the national oil company that they talked about; on the contrary, they immediately tore down the hotel and erected a shipwreck of a garage in its stead. After all the chips had fallen, Kubota didn't get the gleaming edifice that would one day be his; he didn't get a market rate rental for his prized land in the Seattle district; and he didn't get a document that would protect his interests from an uncertain future. What he did get was a forty-year lease with no rental escalations and an ugly, decaying pile of concrete at the end of it all. It was, not surprisingly, a most unfortunate lease.

## WHO KNEW WHAT, WHEN?

Now, the question of whether Kubota knew all along what the Bruce Second and James Corporation had planned to build on Boren's Block One is an interesting one. Only H. T. himself knew for sure, but the plentiful anecdotal evidence indicates that he thought a six-story building was to be built there; Kubota associates and relatives said so, local newspaper stories glowingly described the development, and even architectural plans submitted to the city of Seattle building department evidenced a grander scheme. Prior to Kubota signing the lease, not one shred of information pinpointed what would be the Sinking Ship Garage—with one notable exception: an entry in the SHBC minute book dated the day before the lease was signed, in which "the president [Kubota] stated that it was the intention of the lessee to tear down the existing building and to build on said property a parking garage and service station." Given this one significant piece of trivia, one could deduce that he did in fact know exactly what would be built; however, as is the case with most disagreements, chances are that both statements are true—that is, he knew that the garage would be built, but he also thought the six-story building would be built as well.

Kubota was not in a strong negotiating position with his property; things were not running smoothly on Boren's Block One. He knew the Seattle Hotel was on its last legs as a result of the temblor of 1949 and that the demolition of his landmark hotel would not be well received by the general public—let alone a razing executed by a "Jap." The Pioneer Square area was in a sorry state, and the retail prospects were not likely to improve soon.

Perhaps the lessee alluded to the larger structure as an inducement for Kubota to enter into the lease (structural submittals to the building department noted the capacity and a scheme to increase the structure's height by several stories at a later date) but was willing to guarantee only that the garage portion would be built initially. Perhaps the plan was to build the building in two stages—first the garage, and then the office building—in which case, prudence would dictate that privately Kubota should report only that the first phase would be built and publicly champion the grander scheme, the collateral benefit being the cover he would receive in the event of a public backlash against the demolition. Conversely, self-interest suggests that the Bruce Second and James Corporation would do the opposite, but it didn't.

Perhaps the minute book was later altered to shield officers or directors from liability (in closely held corporations, minutes were rarely typed up and formalized on the day they were recorded).

Whichever set of facts best describes what really happened—the inability of the lessee to complete its stated intent, a simple miscommunication, or a complete deception on the part of one or both parties—the results were the same: a sinking ship of a garage.

## SO, WHAT'S A LEASE WORTH?

Landlords know that leases aren't worth the paper they're written on, but to tenants, that is another matter. For example, this lease was worth a fortune to the tenant—or $2 million, to be more precise, since this was the price paid to the Bruce Second and James Corporation by the Smith Tower group in 1986 (or, stated more correctly, paid to the twelve successors-in-interest of the then-dissolved corporation). It was a staggering price for a fourteen-year leasehold interest.

If someone had asked what you could buy with $2 million in Pioneer Square around that time, the answer would have been simple: any building you want (and the land, too). The only transactions occurring at that time were sales through foreclosure or receiverships. The whole Pioneer Square area from Columbia Street south to King Street was redlined (the illegal practice of refusing to underwrite loans in a district) by the local banks, due to the horrendous losses they had suffered in the Square, and when banks aren't lending, folks don't buy. Due to plummeting real estate values, bank debt on properties was exceeding market value, with very few exceptions.

Thus, if there were any interested buyers out there, they wisely waited for the owners to default on their loans and then bought the properties once the banks had written down (or written off) their loans. For example, four years later (1990) in a greatly improved market, Commonwealth (my company) purchased a newly rehabilitated twenty-four-unit apartment building with ground floor retail and mezzanine office for $1.5 million. In this sale, the owner of the land (it was ground leased as well) got nothing, the owners of the building lost all their investment, and the bank got to write down its loan.

As a further example, a decade later, in 1995, the same Smith Tower group lost the landmark in foreclosure after ten abysmal years of losing money. The lender, General Electric Credit Equities, took the property back in a trustee's sale for the accrued debt of $11.5 million and then sold it one year later at a $4 million loss. Times were tough, and losing was a way of life in and around Boren's Block One.

So, in summary, while Kubota was getting $1,500 a month for his half-acre property in downtown Seattle, in 1986 the Bruce Second and James Corporation got $2 million for their lease that had just fourteen years to run. This is all one needs to know in determining how favorable Kubota's 1960 lease was to his tenant. For Commonwealth's small part in the transaction, which amounted to little more than some paper shuffling, we received a fee roughly equal to what Kubota would have received in rent over the next four years.

## KUBOTA AND MIMBU PART COMPANY

At the first meeting of SHBC shareholders in 1968, just months after the repeal of the Alien Land Law in Washington State, Henry and Easter Kubota became the sole shareholders of the SHBC. In what must have been a miraculous alignment of the stars, each and every one of the baby-faced *nisei* had simultaneously agreed to tender their shares to Kubota and resign from the board of directors. With the exception of the nonshareholding Mimbu, who continued on as secretary and in-house counsel, they were no longer needed.

In 1971, Mimbu set up the HTK Management Company for Kubota, the purpose of which was to serve as a "property management officer" for the SHBC; in return, the management company earned 10 percent of the gross rents received by the corporation, and Kubota avoided double taxation—that is, tax at the corporate level *and* the personal level (from the corporate dividends he would receive)—on the bulk of his income.

The two men might have plotted, schemed, and gotten rich forever had it not been for a falling out in 1977. The exact nature of the disagreement is unclear, but one fact is not in question: Mimbu switched teams.

The letterhead for Mimbu's missives began reading "Franco, Asia, Bensussen, and Coe" instead of "Mimbu and Wong," as it had since 1950. Kubota's attorney had gone to work for the lawyer that had negotiated the ground lease on behalf of the enemy (said lawyer being a significant stockholder of Bruce Second and James Corporation as well).

Was not the former firm the agent of deceit? Was not the first-titled attorney, Franco, a member of the Bruce Second and James Corporation that delivered H. T. Kubota his greatest failure as a businessman? How could Mimbu do this? His new partners weren't Japanese—they weren't even Chinese.

In a very tersely worded resolution adopted at a special meeting of the shareholders of the SHBC in December 1977, William Y. Mimbu was immediately removed as a director and an officer of the corporation and replaced with people whose loyalty was beyond reproach: wife Easter and son Thomas Minoru Kubota. Four months later, a new Kubota attorney, Douglas Palmer Jr., of the law firm Foster, Pepper and Riviera, filed a statement of intent to dissolve SHBC. Palmer birthed a new general partnership, HTK Management Ltd., which absorbed the assets of SHBC. The memory of William Mimbu could now be erased forever—or so H. T. thought.

## Transforming Pioneer Square

In the early 1980s, the birthplace of Seattle had been left behind by city leaders to rot and decay, and so had the souls for whom modern society has no place—and these people all called the streets and doorways of Pioneer Square their home. The vast majority of the city's human service agencies were clustered in the area, and the clients of same would never be confused for Seattle's best and brightest. It was a depressed and depressing place to be, where all the worst that man has wrought was on agonizing display. Very few members of the brokerage community chose to work this charming little submarket, which suffered a much higher vacancy rate than downtown Seattle as a whole.

The Economic Reform and Tax Act (ERTA) of 1980 offered to all owners of capital a basket full of goodies, two of which happened to be a 25 percent investment tax credit for rehabilitation expenditures of historic structures and a greatly accelerated depreciation schedule of those expenditures. This was good news for the old buildings of Pioneer Square, but it was Reaganomics at its worst: investors rushed in to take advantage of supply-side tax incentives with little regard for the trivia of the investments—such as whether everybody else was doing the same thing.

Scores of limited partnerships were soon syndicated with the specific intent of rehabilitating the Richardsonian-Romanesque structures of the Pioneer Square Historic District and transforming them into office buildings. Preservationists praised the adaptive reuse of the buildings, but the investors cared only that it was a tax shelter. The tiny Pioneer Square office market went from 200,000 square feet to more than 1 million square feet in twenty-four months, and the resulting bloodbath concluded with most investors losing both their money and their tax credits.

The greater Seattle office market, just as in all the major cities across the country in the mid-1980s, fared no better in this rapid expansion, experiencing double-digit vacancies and plummeting rental rates. The national supply of office space had grown so dramatically over the previous five years that pundits speculated correctly that it would take nearly a decade for business growth to absorb the glut. One Asian investor, when asked during a TV interview about his marketing plan to fill his empty fifty-story skyscraper in Houston, retorted plaintively, "Marketing plan? Who need marketing plan? I need tenant!" There was simply no one to fill all the space.

## THE SINKING SHIP GARAGE: NO SIMPLE SOLUTION

Sharks and real estate brokers are basically lazy; whether it is food or fees they seek, they will rarely pursue an opportunity if any significant obstacle is apparent. This was good news for my company, Commonwealth, since the Pioneer Square real estate market of the early 1980s presented several significant obstacles. Sharks occasionally would swim down to the Square, but they never hung around for long; the meals were easier and tastier uptown.

In June 1986, the new owners of the Smith Tower had hired Commonwealth to try to find tenants for their building, and in addition to the glut of office space, they had one other problem: a decided lack of parking for said tenants. For any real estate broker, lazy or not, who cared to look, it was plain to see that the solution to the Smith Tower's parking problem was sitting across the street, on Boren's Block One. The simplicity of this solution was not lost on Commonwealth's Douglas Graham, and he immediately set about assembling a sales package on the Sinking Ship Garage to present to our client.

The first step in assembling such a package is to determine the landowner, which most brokers sheepishly ask someone else, typically a title company, to do. The owner of Boren's Block One was, remember, identified as the Seattle Hotel Building Corporation, which had purchased the property in 1941. Yet there was also a recorded ground lease on the land in which SHBC had leased the entire property to the Bruce Second and James Corporation for forty years, beginning in 1960 and slated to end on March 31, 2000. Graham quickly deduced that his deal would not be as easy as he had originally thought, since Bruce Second and James Corporation would control the property for at least the next fourteen years (and possibly thirty-four years, since the lease had those two ten-year extension options), at which time the property would then revert to SHBC (later, HTK Management LLC).

A clean and simple sale of the land was out of the question, so the only way to solve the Smith Tower's immediate parking problem was to make some sort of deal with the Bruce Second and James Corporation to acquire their leasehold interest. Further complicating the mission of the fee-seeking broker were three facts:

(1) The Bruce Second and James Corporation had dissolved some four years earlier, and its successor-in-interest was now twelve individuals.

(2) There was a long-term lease with a parking operator, Ampco Parking, that was effectively managing the property for those twelve individuals.

(3) Most importantly, collecting a fee in the midst of this landless morass of a transaction would be tricky—after all, we were real estate brokers, not shoe salesmen.

It was enough to make any self-respecting shark swim away.

## 1986: BRUCE SECOND AND JAMES CORPORATION SELLS ITS GROUND LEASE

The Smith Tower group that ended up purchasing the leasehold interest in the Sinking Ship Garage from the Bruce Second and James Corporation initially called themselves the Rokan Corporation—the name being a contracted spelling of the lead partner, Robert Kantor; however, shortly before closing the deal, the group decided to take title in the name of Financial Center Investors. FCI had been formed two years earlier as a California limited partnership—Kantor was a general partner—and had been registered in Washington State the week of closing.

To further confuse matters, unbeknownst to many who were party to the transaction (including me), the entity that first took title to the leasehold interest, prior to FCI, was a firm called C. A. C. Company, a California limited partnership that had a general partner by the name of Investor Services Inc. (whose president was Robert Kantor). The transfers from the Bruce Second and James Corporation to C. A. C. Company and then to FCI were simultaneous transactions with consecutive recording numbers occurring on December 16, 1986. Investor Services Inc. was later replaced with Enutrof Inc. ("fortune" spelled backward).

Later still, FCI transferred the interest to Rokan Partners, a California general partnership, which later added an Idaho limited partnership also called Rokan Partners, which named Rokan Corporation, the same Delaware corporation that originally was to buy the leasehold interest, as its general partner.

Sound confusing? Well, it was supposed to be.

Robert Kantor was an ambitious attorney who knew how to make money and, better yet, how to use the law so as not to lose it; he set up a labyrinth of legal entities to make, among other things, a creditor's attempts to collect a debt an exhaustive and futile exercise. The specific purposes of all these legal machinations rest only in the busy mind of Kantor; however, tax avoidance and limitation of personal liability were surely a couple of the chief aims (and perhaps some fee extraction from his partners as well).

His lender on the project, Seattle-First National Bank, did not consent to the relay-race transfers that Kantor had made—and may not have known of them—until nearly two years after the fact. Most remarkable in this whole mess was the fact that Seattle-First National (then owned by Bank of America) not only lent Kantor the entire purchase price but also chipped in an extra $100,000 to make improvements to the garage! They made this bizarre commitment at a time when every lender in Pioneer Square was upside-down on its loans—that is, having more loan than value—and on a leasehold interest to boot! Perhaps they decided it was better to *begin* with a bad loan than to be surprised later on.

Early on in his career, Kantor learned three financial truths: (1) money never sleeps; (2) buildings work even if you don't; and (3) billable hours are a lousy way to make an "enutrof." He was a lawyer and a deal maker who observed correctly that the landmark tower and garage possessed the three critical elements of real estate holdings—location, location, and location—owing to their position in the heart of the government, transportation, and entertainment sectors of town. When paired with the seemingly minuscule price being asked for the landmark Smith Tower and the ERTA package of tax goodies provided by President Reagan, Kantor felt certain he had a sure thing.

At this point, Kantor proudly owned both the Smith Tower (or, more accurately, controlled the partnership that owned it) and the Sinking Ship Garage (but not the sorry lot upon which it rested). Like many investors from outside Seattle who have rushed in to take advantage of the apparent bargains in Pioneer Square, Kantor was also unaware of some relevant trivia surrounding his investment. He was feeling pretty good about his investments and planned on sitting back and watching the money roll in. But there is another maxim in real estate—Pioneer Square real estate, that is—which observes that when the out-of-towners show up, the time has come to sell.

Boren's Block One was certainly no exception ...

# Chapter 5:
# *Nisei*

In 2000, John Fujii, Henry Kubota's son-in-law by virtue of his marriage to Kubota's daughter Doris in 1959, was embroiled in a dispute (and subsequent lawsuit) with Robert Kantor over the proper rent to be charged for Boren's Block One during the first of the two ground lease term extensions. Fujii had managed HTK Management LLC (and its predecessor, HTK Management Ltd.) for more than a decade and by all accounts had done a most credible job. Doris Kubota Fujii had in many ways selected a man not unlike her father.

John Fujii was intelligent, trusting, and unassuming, and he possessed an instantly recognizable integrity. A 1957 graduate of the University of Washington, Fujii majored in forestry, which he followed up with a master's degree in forest products in 1959. He was a member of a learned family whose members all held postgraduate degrees, an educational pedigree of which he was quite proud. Still hungry for knowledge, though, he decided to pick up stakes and move his new wife across the country to enter a doctorate program in environmental forestry, which was offered by the State University of New York but located at Syracuse University; a few years later, in 1964, he brought his family back home to the Northwest with a Ph.D. from both institutions.

Fujii humbly met the familial obligations with an attentive and measured persistence that, as the years went by, ended up consuming a good deal of his time. He did not choose the real estate industry as his passion but was instead drawn into it through an obligation to family as well as his father-in-law's considerable holdings.

Fujii was *nisei*, the American-born son of a Japanese immigrant who had come to America in 1923 as a timber buyer to aid his native country's efforts to rebuild Tokyo after the Great Kanto Earthquake of the same year. Fujii's maternal grandfather had immigrated to America at the turn of the twentieth century (so in one aspect, he could be considered *sansei*—third generation), so his American roots ran relatively deep. Like all *nisei*, he had been incarcerated in an internment camp during World War II, where he experienced firsthand the illegal actions of an overreaching government. He had felt the sting of exclusion and bigotry in the only homeland he had ever known and held a healthy skepticism of bureaucrats and their motives. Fujii possessed many admirable personal traits and combined them with a full life experience—two considerable assets that would, unfortunately, betray him in the next major disaster to befall Boren's Block One.

The lawsuit with Kantor notwithstanding, things were looking pretty good. The transformational moment in time that the Kubota family had been eagerly anticipating—when the cursed ground lease would finally expire—was fast approaching, which would return the prized land back to the family's possession and use. Kantor was making his life difficult, but the welcome and long-awaited safe harbor was finally in view. Evolution was in the air and champagne was chilling.

Alas, good news has always been short-lived on Boren's Block One, and now a new obstacle loomed on the horizon. A major transportation project was threatening to condemn Boren's Block One for the public good: the Seattle Monorail Project, a uniquely Seattle mass transit solution, had its eye on the Sinking Ship Garage as a likely candidate for a monorail station.

After sixty years of foul weather on the sinking ship that was Boren's Block One—world war, internment, earthquakes, corruption, bigotry, urban decay, deception, lawsuits—now this. In the wake of this new threat, Fujii was determined not to be the pilot to finally lose this dubious prize after all its stormy years at sea. Nonetheless, he was now forced to acknowledge two inescapable truths: (1) after sixty years, he might lose his family's land for a monorail station, and (2) Kantor would under no circumstances fail to extend his lease. The parade of tragedies marched on ...

{ THE SEATTLE MONORAIL: BELOVED WORLD'S FAIR ICON

The city of Seattle has long had a love affair with the monorail, beginning with the Seattle World's Fair in 1962. Organized to showcase a city entering and embracing the twenty-first century, the World's Fair was run by an entity known as the Century 21 Exposition, Inc., which sought any and all things futuristic to highlight its technological theme. Ford Motor Company sponsored an exhibit dubbed the "Adventure in Outer Space," and the Boeing Company funded something called a "Spacearium," but the two most recognizable icons of the World's Fair were the 605-foot-tall Space Needle and the Alweg Monorail.

Designed and 100 percent financed by Swedish sister firm Alwac International, the trains and controls for the Seattle Center monorail were fabricated in Germany to run on the 1.3-mile track built by local firm Howard S. Wright Construction Inc. at a cost just over $3 million The souvenir program for the World's Fair described the monorail thus:

> The two slim white rails, narrowing in unison toward infinity, skim over the noise and the clutter of street traffic ... Slowly at first, then faster, the light aluminum train glides from Westlake Station, its eight drive wheels and thirty-two guide wheels clutching its own monorail. Four cars tandem bend into the curve above Stewart Street and ahead is the straightaway, a mile of unswerving concrete beam. The driver accelerates and four electric motors suck in power. Twenty miles per hour ... forty ... sixty ... seventy. Down the other monorail the second train appears and speeds forward then swishes past in an amazingly quiet rush. At eye level, the colonnade of trees along Fifth Avenue appears as a blur of foliage and the buildings flicker past like a picket fence. The driver decelerates and the motors brake for the Denny Way curve. The monorail train eases over the crowds and

across the fence and slips into Century 21 Station. One hundred twenty-five persons rise from their seats and step out to enjoy the Seattle World's Fair. The elapsed time from downtown—ninety-five seconds.

The Seattle monorail's first year of operation was a triumph, and also its best year, with ridership exceeding 3 million passenger trips. This success liquidated all debt associated with the monorail's construction in 365 days—a truly inconceivable notion today: that a transit system could pay for itself that quickly.

Alweg, which had big plans for its monorail, viewed the Century 21 monorail as a necessary promotional expense. The tiny Seattle project was just an appetizer in anticipation of the main course: a comprehensive proposal to link all the communities of Los Angeles with a network of monorails. The Swedes touted the success of Seattle's monorail and offered Los Angelesians a chance to meet the future with a forty-three-mile system that would link the San Fernando Valley, the Wilshire corridor, the San Bernardino corridor, and downtown Los Angeles. Alwac would build and finance the $105 million monorail, turning over a completed and operational system to the city without a penny of civic investment or obligation—save the fare revenue to retire the debt. City planners were excited with the prospect, but unfortunately the monorail proposal was quietly quashed in back-room deals by the all-powerful automotive and petroleum interests—notably Standard Oil—before ever saturating the public's awareness. Injured mortally by these and other failed ventures, the Alweg monorail company dissolved soon thereafter.

## THE MONORAIL GROWS UP

Three years after the 1962 World's Fair and the unveiling of Seattle's cutting-edge Alweg Monorail, the Century 21 Exposition sold the system to the city of Seattle, which later turned over operational responsibility to Metro Transit Authority (now a part of King County). The Washington State Legislature had created Metro in 1958, but up until the early 1960s, Metro had jurisdiction only for water quality and waste treatment. The enabling legislation had inserted mass transit to the list of Metro's responsibilities but conditioned its official inclusion on a public vote. In the mid-1960s, King County set that vote in motion, offering a referendum to authorize Metro Transit to undertake planning for a regional mass transit system. The referendum faced a well-financed campaign by the American Automobile Association (AAA)—no doubt with the assistance of gasoline purveyors—that accused Metro of many devious plans, one of which was a "wheel tax" that would basically tax anything that moved. Not surprisingly, the referendum was crushed.

Nonetheless, Seattle's monorail was a state-of-the-art system. Alweg International had incorporated highly advanced speed and stopping control systems, which monitored the train's performance on various parts of the track as well as its approach to the station platforms. These systems—or "governors"—ensured smooth and safe operation for the system's first years by basically making the trains idiot-proof; even a drunk monkey could drive them. City (and, later, Metro) drivers, who select their routes based on seniority, always left the assignment of the monorail to rookie drivers because being captain of these trains was the equivalent of being commander-in-chief of a flashlight. The trains were either on or off—little skill or cunning was required.

But sometime after the city took ownership of the monorail, the governors were decommissioned for some unknown reason—perhaps because of lack of replacement parts, or maybe because they made the trains no fun to drive. Unfortunately, once the governors were removed, some skill and cunning were required to drive the monorail, and so trouble began and the era of safe monorail operation was officially over. Other bad news for the Seattle monorail was that a good deal of its operating and engineering information, which was in German, was lost when Alweg dissolved, leaving local operators without most of the original specifications in any language—the technological equivalent of handing a stone-age man the keys to a Cadillac and asking him to maintain it properly. A series of incidents, in combination with other factors—significant operating losses and a federal grant audit demanding competitive bids being two—induced the city to put the operations contract out to bid in 1994.

The only bidder to respond to the city's request for proposal was Seattle Monorail Services Inc. (SMSI), a local firm that was owned in part by the private group that owned the Space Needle. Thankfully, for the taxpayers of Seattle, Metro was now out of the monorail business and SMSI was in.

Under private operation, the monorail enjoyed a resurgence. Many elements of the monorail's glorious past returned—most notably, system profitability. Instead of feeding the mono-monster with piles of cash on a monthly basis, the city began feasting on the monorail's success, due to a renegotiation of the SMSI management contract, which provided the city a one-half share of the not insignificant profits. All went well as the trains and the calendar rolled into the long-awaited twenty-first century for Seattle's icon, which was, and is, the last operating Alweg monorail system in existence.

## 1997: PLANNING A MONORAIL EXPANSION— THE FIRST YES VOTE

Buoyed by financial success, the monorail's red and blue trains quietly swooshing over Fifth Avenue downtown began to enjoy cult status as well. Seattle cab driver Dick Falkenbury, the principal visionary of a plan to expand monorail service within the city, observed the profitability of the existing monorail and its prominent operators (SMSI's owners included the family of Howard S. Wright, whose construction firm had built the monorail track for the World's Fair). Falkenbury concluded that a citywide monorail system was the best transit solution for Seattle and that private money would rain down from the heavens in support of such a plan.

In November 1997, the Seattle electorate was set to vote on Initiative 41, which proposed construction of the second generation of monorail service—an X-shaped system connecting the four corners of the city with the downtown core. If it were approved, the initiative would establish the Elevated Transportation Company (ETC), give it $200,000 seed money, and authorize it to seek private investment for the construction of a forty-mile elevated transit system. "Rise above it all" was the sound bite for the commuter set.

The plan enjoyed tremendous grassroots support—owing to the nostalgia of the old monorail and a general frustration over Seattle's dismal traffic situation; however, it did not fare as well among the purveyors of capital that Falkenbury sought to attract. The old guard and the mass transit wonks were wary of the plan (it wasn't theirs) and its sponsor (a cabbie who might have watched a few too many episodes of *Star Trek*), thus most chose to stay on the sideline for the first round. To their dismay, when the votes were counted, a 53 percent majority had approved the monorail proposal, and suddenly Falkenbury and his fellow monorailiens, preaching mono to a stereo world, were the talk of the town.

This "mandate from the commons" was also met with great skepticism in the halls of power, due to the fact that its intents were not only unfunded but also perceived as unnecessary, due to the light rail system already in the works at the time. Seattle, like many major American cities, had been waging the mass transit wars for nearly four decades—a battle that was finally resolved in 1996 when voters in neighboring King, Pierce, and Snohomish counties agreed to raise their taxes to fund a $4 billion plan to design and build a regional light rail system to link the major cities of greater Puget Sound—said system dubbed Sound Transit. Bureaucrats doubted there was sufficient civic will and resources to build two transit systems simultaneously and decided to let the monorail expansion idea die a slow and unnatural death in the clutches of the glacially slow Seattle political process. After two years, with the seed money gone and no private pennies from heaven in sight, the ETC hibernated.

## 2000: The Second Yes Vote

Monorail boosters, angered by the politicians' indifference to their dream and skeptical of Sound Transit's ability to actually build a light rail system, quickly moved to remedy the situation with a new proposal that would breathe life into ETC with a $6 million cash infusion and a two-year window to come up with a plan to put before the electorate. Initiative 53, the second vote on the monorail, which gave ETC the time and money it needed, was approved by 55 percent of Seattle voters in November 2000, and now Falkenbury and his $6 million suddenly had more friends than he ever thought possible. Folks from all over Seattle, who had so far been happy just to sit on the sidelines and watch the action, quickly snapped on their chinstraps and got into the game.

In October 2001, a group of three former fence-sitters (and now ETC board members)—an SMSI principal (Stuart Rolfe), a former Seattle city councilmember (Tom Weeks), and a public sector consultant turned developer (Joel Horn)—joined one of the leading monorailiens (Peter Sherwin) for a trip to Tokyo to see a big-city monorail in action. The group's trip was sponsored by a sister company to Hitachi Monorail, Mitsui, the manufacturer of six Japanese monorails currently in service, in the hopes of convincing the Seattleites that only one company and one country truly had the wherewithal to make Seattle's monorail expansion a reality: Hitachi and (ironically, as it turns out for Boren's Block One) Japan.

As they planned and plotted among themselves about how to create the greatest transit system in American history, this visionary group appeared to be airborne before even boarding the plane. Voters had given them the "green light" and plenty of "green" to go solve a city's transit problem, and they felt the strength of a million-man mandate, which coursed through their veins like a noxious drug. As they energetically brainstormed in the Red Carpet lounge at Seattle-Tacoma International Airport before their flight to Tokyo, they pondered their drawings on city maps using colored pens, and from said sketches they baptized their creation the "Green Line."

While none in attendance would admit to naming it so, the four men saw nothing but green ahead for their project, in every sense of the word, as far as the eye could see. Falkenbury's X would soon lose both its eastern arms, but the fourteen-mile Green Line was a plan with legs.

From this point, the ETC moved at light speed with the guidance of just a few stars. The three reformed fence-sitters, who had known each other prior to the formation of ETC, were young, bright, ambitious, and mostly distrustful of public process—especially the endless Seattle variety. The public-sector-consultant-turned-developer, Joel Horn, had received a civic spanking in 1995 at the hands of the voters, who shot down the "Seattle Commons" project, a mixed-use development that he had directed, centered around a seventy-acre park connecting the central business district with nearby Lake Union. Backed by the mayor, the media, and $20 million from Microsoft cofounder and billionaire Paul Allen, this grassroots proposal was handily defeated on several counts—cost and small-business displacement being the two elements most often cited; however, some insiders who spoke out of earshot of a microphone cited the project's director and his hubris as a primary source of failure.

Upon conclusion of the trip to Japan, Horn resigned from the ETC board so as to permit his acceptance of a staff position to direct and implement the monorail plan. The former councilman and the SMSI principal stayed behind on the board to give him the access and resources he needed, and the "group of three" determined that they would show Seattle how to build a billion-dollar transit system not in a few decades, but in just a few years.

The need for speed would prove to be a mistake many times over. Perfect hindsight shows that the first error took the form of a decision made early in the game not to seek state or federal funds to finance the project. An application for federal funds would create many problems for the entrepreneurial team at the monorail—principally, subordination to yet more levels of government bureaucracy and broader electorates. Delays and shifting political winds were the last things the group of three wanted, so they settled on a citywide levy of the motor vehicle excise tax (MVET) to fund their monorail (while the MVET is technically a state tax, it is levied locally). This approach had the advantage of needing only local approval by the Seattle electorate of the tax levy, but carried the downside of needing to go back to the voters in the event the MVET proved insufficient. The MVET estimates that were provided to the ETC board seemed more than adequate to finance the budgeted costs, so in the interests of expediency, the choice was made to narrow their political risk to the sleepy confines of Seattle proper.

## 2002: THE THIRD YES VOTE

The third public vote in support of the monorail's Green Line project came in November 2002. In this proposition, Citizen Petition No. 1, the developing entity of the project, the ETC, was succeeded by the Seattle Popular Monorail Authority, more commonly known as the Seattle Monorail Project (SMP). In the aftermath of the passage of Citizen Petition No. 1, the SMP was granted the authority "to plan, acquire, build, finance and operate a city monorail system pursuant to the plan adopted by the Elevated Transportation Company (predecessor to the SMP) on August 5, 2002. The authority can levy an annual special excise tax not to exceed 1.4 percent on the value of every motor vehicle owned by a Seattle resident for the privilege of using a motor vehicle and issue not more than $1.5 billion in bonds for an initial line and second-line planning." The ETC's original plan was cut from forty miles to just fourteen and ran from West Seattle up to the Ballard neighborhood—presumably so the aging steel pensioners in West Seattle could easily go visit their Ballard fishing buddies. The money began rolling in right away by way of the MVET, and implementation of the plan began in earnest. Finally.

Immediately after the 2002 election, John Fujii decided to be proactive and contacted the ETC to find out what plans there were for his family's property: Boren's Block One. By this time, Fujii knew the preliminary monorail routing was down Second Avenue and that, given the density of historic (and hence untouchable) structures in the immediate vicinity, the Sinking Ship Garage was a likely station candidate.

These initial discussions were strained because the ETC didn't have much to say at that time and expressed even less. If the station was to be located on Fujii's land, it seemed there was little he could do but try to make the best of a bad set of circumstances. Fujii's approach to the problem was very Japanese—that is, to a large extent, he accepted his fate. *Shikata-ga-nai*, or "it can't be helped," was the attitude taken by his *issei* forebears during their internment in World War II, and to him this situation seemed to demand a similar mind-set.

This was difficult, however, since condemnation of the property, assuming any reasonable price, was not an attractive option for HTK. Under the ground lease, in the event of condemnation, the award proceeds were to be distributed as follows: (1) the lessor (HTK) would receive the share that was attributable to the land; (2) the lessee (Rokan Partners) would receive the share that was attributable to the leasehold interest; and (3) the two would share any award relating to the improvements in the ratio that the unexpired term of the lease—including option periods—related to the full term (sixty years).

Although on its face this division might seem fair and equitable, if one examines the value a condemnation award might generate in 1986, one can readily see that a fee interest generating $1,500 per month would command a small fraction of the award (maybe $200,000) compared to the leasehold interest that already has been shown to be worth ten times that sum ($2 million). The ground lease was rearing its ugly head again, and it looked as though the good guys would again finish last. Attorneys and appraisers would no doubt litigate the matter for years in order to assign the relative values, but at the end of the day, the lease was listing mightily in favor of the lessee, and the end result would be unfavorable for HTK.

While the taking by eminent domain was certainly a problem, Fujii saw also a collateral opportunity. For more than forty years, this ground lease had been the proverbial fly in his ointment, and this fly had potentially twenty more years of life. Surely, he would lose a portion of the property for the station, but if he could somehow engage the cooperation of SMP, perhaps he could get them to mortally wound the pesky insect—lose some land but at the same time lose a ground lease. He decided his plan would be to try and work a deal with SMP whereby the transit authority would condemn only the leasehold interest and in return he would agree to give them whatever they wanted. He would stipulate that they would need the land for the station and the construction staging if he could keep what was left after all was said and done. This approach had myriad advantages to HTK, the most important two being that (1) he could ultimately retain some of the family property and (2) he could avoid the adverse allocation of the condemnation award that the ground lease would dictate. It was a decent plan.

Not long after the monorail financing decision was cast in stone via Citizen Petition No.1, the pace of the MVET receipts were found to be seriously lagging against the projections, to the tune of 30 percent below the original estimates. The 2003 SMP budget was amended twice in board resolutions, and the budget for 2004 (which was "realigned" once as well) now only displayed a detailed expense spreadsheet and made no estimate as to revenue (said MVET receipts). The SMP board-approved 2005 budget was just one line.

According to Joel Horn, there were three primary reasons for the problem: (1) evasion—many residents began licensing their BMWs and Mercedes to addresses outside the city limits to avoid the annual 1.4 percent tax ($700 per year for a $50,000 car); (2) the state Department of Licensing was not applying the MVET to out-of-state cars coming into Seattle; and (3) the estimates were made with an unhealthy reliance on borrowed Sound Transit projections, which allegedly included automobiles and other personal property not located within the city limits in Seattle's MVET numbers (this was supposedly done by Sound Transit in an effort to bully Seattle city officials into supporting the larger regional plan).

Some blamed the state for providing just plain bad numbers, and, of course, there was the inevitable faction that always accuses whoever is in charge—in this case, the SMP finance committee and its consultant—with either intentional deception, sheer incompetence, or all three (citing the maxim that there are only three types of bureaucratic prognosticators, and both are bad at math). Whatever the combination of elements that ultimately caused the rosy view of projections, the end result was that the project team faced a critical funding shortfall.

Heartache number two arrived soon afterward when the construction budget was revised upward 15 percent. Now there was a 45 percent funding gap, which optimism and entrepreneurial spirit could hardly be expected to fill. In true real estate developer fashion, the 800-pound gorilla in the room was regularly and faithfully ignored while the exuberant team forged ahead, extolling the virtues of the monorail technology.

In fairness, this sort of approach is often a necessary condition in the world of real estate development, especially development of complex municipal projects, since many variables are often being resolved simultaneously. For example, it is complicated to project passenger fares for a proposed system when the basic elements of the system—route, construction costs, financing issues—are in a constant state of flux. Fierce headwinds notwithstanding, the word out of the monorail office was something to the effect of "Trust us, people, we know what we're doing. Let us worry about the details. We will resolve the issues in the most advantageous way for the city and its people."

## USING EMINENT DOMAIN TO BOLSTER REVENUE

In the context of these shortfalls, the newly formed inner circle of the monorail board (the SMSI principal resigned from the SMP board, since the proposed Green Line was going to put SMSI out of business) needed to find some solutions and generate some additional revenue. Officially, Horn declared that the 30 percent revenue gap was "not a significant problem" because "the [MVET] growth has been on a stronger track than we [originally] projected. We'll actually end up possibly having actually more revenue for the project over the time frame, not less ..."

Privately, the situation was dire. Construction costs would need to be cut, and nightly prayers were invoked to apply downward pressure on interest rates. SMP was perched on a slippery slope, and short of fraudulent activities, the only potent weapons left in their limited arsenal were (1) the ability to limit the scope of the project and (2) the power of condemnation. Certainly, steps were taken to reduce the project scope (the fourteen-mile Green Line was later reduced to ten miles), but so too was the second bullet, the sovereign power of eminent domain, put into use.

A fact not unnoticed by the SMP brass was the conclusion of another very public condemnation case that had come before the Washington Supreme Court in 1998—Washington State Convention and Trade Center v. Evans. The central issue in this case involved the proposed expansion of the Convention Center, for which the state legislature had appropriated $111 million, conditioned on the Convention Center pitching in $15 million of its own monies.

The Convention Center developed a plan that involved condemning property across the street from the existing Convention Center; however, the expansion space they sought would sit four stories above street level and be accessed from the existing space across the street via a skybridge. Once the property was condemned, the land and three floors below the expansion space were to be immediately sold to a private developer that in turn would contribute the required $15 million for the privilege and build the shell of the expansion space for them.

A neat deal, and despite the best efforts of the condemnee (Evans) to fight this taking for what she felt was mostly a private use, the Supremes upheld the order of public use and necessity decreed by the lower court, determining that the condemnation involved a public use as defined by the Washington State Constitution. The court observed that the proposed property condemned was within the "footprint" of the space that was determined necessary for the public use (the expansion space) and that the private development contemplated on the three floors below was "merely incidental." The SMP folks took note.

Nineteen monorail stations were planned. Nineteen times $15 million per station is a pretty big number ($285 million, to be precise), and since the stations would mostly "rise above it all" (elevated in the air), SMP figured it could probably enjoy some construction contributions as well (as the Convention Center had). Granted, the likelihood of SMP garnering that kind of money for each of the nineteen stations was unlikely, but nonetheless this model offered a very lucrative opportunity for a forward-thinking agency. Thus, it also stands to reason that, mathematically speaking, revenue shortfalls plus eminent domain power equaled a liberal interpretation of the land needed for the stations, coupled with the need for clear and concise development policies on the part of the SMP.

The first set of policies, a comprehensive thirteen-page document that spelled out in detail the myriad procedures SMP would employ, was adopted just after the 2002 yes vote. One year later, after the SMP's 2003 and 2004 budgets had experienced repeated massaging due to the MVET problems, the monorail board adopted an amendment to those policies, which detailed something called "integrated development" and who qualified for it. Integrated development, wherein third-party development would be concurrent with a monorail station and part and parcel of the station, was a public-private partner strategy likely devised straight out of the 1998 Washington State Convention and Trade Center v. Evans decision. Another tool, "associated development," involved the sale or lease of excess SMP condemned land to a third party after station construction was complete and gave SMP a vehicle to realize the increase in value of neighboring parcels brought about by its public investment.

These policies were two clearly defined strategies contained in the SMP guidelines that were developed to reduce the overall cost of the project—not some obscure principles that some wonk threw in the works with the standard boilerplate. Once more, Horn himself allowed as how "Well, we've looked at all nineteen stations in terms of, you know, is this a possible integrated or associated development ..." There was a staff position in the SMP Right-of-Way Department for the express purpose of pursuing the opportunities that integrated and associated development presented—and they were presenting themselves regularly.

One such integrated development was already in the works for a station near the Pike Place Market. It involved property controlled by a former board member of the defunct Seattle Commons project—one of Horn's old bosses (William Justen)—who just happened to be a real estate developer and former head of the city's Department of Construction and Land Use. Even worse, the monorail plan that was put before the electorate in 2002 as Citizens' Petition No. 1 had a conceptual drawing of that particular integrated development on the front cover—the front cover, mind you.

## SMP EYES BOREN'S BLOCK ONE

John Fujii was well aware of the integrated development that was being touted very publicly at the Pike Place Market, and he smelled a rat. Meetings with developer Justen had been going on for months, but the monorail wouldn't give Fujii the time of day. As the Kubotas' luck would have it, the owner of the landmark Smith Tower (it had been purchased from the lender who had foreclosed on Kantor) was also controlled by Justen. Fujii was convinced that Horn was planning to reproduce the development contemplated at the Pike Place Market station on his property and toss another bone to his former Seattle Commons boss (who would surely be in need of parking for his Smith Tower tenants postcondemnation). Fujii's plan to keep some land and derail the ground lease would be thwarted if SMP chose to work with Justen instead of HTK, since full condemnation would be required to sell the remaining property to a third party. Fujii had stiff competition, and he knew it. Nonetheless, he proceeded in good faith to talk to SMP about the future of his property in hopes of making some headway.

In the limited discussions that began in February 2003, which were always through counsel, HTK allowed as how it was willing to sell SMP the land needed for the monorail station but was interested in the possibility of pursuing an integrated or associated development on the site. Fujii said he knew of the station's limited footprint and had heard in the community outreach meetings that many ideas were being tossed around for the unused property—parks, affordable housing, mixed-use, et cetera.

Fujii patiently detailed to SMP his family's long and tortured association with the storied property and their nostalgic desire to retain any portion of it that they could, while at the same time saying HTK wanted to assist in the creation of this important civic asset that was to be the Green Line. He would gladly give SMP their station site but wanted to ensure that if there was any third-party development to be done, it would be HTK doing that developing and not somebody else. Even though Boren's Block One had been little more than trouble to everyone ever involved with it, the Kubota clan stubbornly clung to it. What would possess them to fight so hard for this troubled parcel is unclear, but, clearly, they were possessed.

Chapter 6:

# Condemnation

Although some introductory dialogue had been ongoing between HTK Management LLC and the Seattle Monorail Project's Right-of-Way Department, officially SMP began its activities with respect to the acquisition of Boren's Block One in April 2003, just days after Resolution 04-12 was adopted by the SMP board establishing the Green Line's alignment and station locations. The Right-of-Way Department's first call was to an attorney. The second one was to hire an appraiser. The property owner, HTK Management LLC—through its manager, John Fujii—was then informed of SMP's intentions for the site (identified as "DT360" by SMP staff) and the forthcoming appraisal and purchase offer. The appraisal was completed six months later, on October 20, and two months subsequent, on December 16, 2003, an offer of $6 million for DT360 was communicated to HTK.

Preliminary station locations and designs had been disseminated to the public by this time, which detailed a few rough components of the proposed Pioneer Square station that was to sit on the Sinking Ship Garage property. The first station design, dated January 7, 2004, showed little more than a platform and a structure (labeled "building," with unspecified uses) that covered the entire site.

The limited conversations between SMP and HTK subsequent to SMP adoption of Resolution 04-12 hastened a flurry of activity on both sides, albeit not with each other, as the respective attorneys began their pre-condemnation-trial posturing. P. Steven DiJulio of Foster Pepper and Shefelman, lead counsel for the petitioner, SMP, immediately marshaled and muzzled his troops in an effort to keep the message consistent. He recognized the hole that HTK was trying to drive its trucks through and, despite the written SMP property acquisition policy (which encouraged simultaneous negotiation and condemnation proceedings), he wanted to halt all discussions regarding joint development with HTK so as not to jeopardize the upcoming condemnation action. There were a lot of monorail voices involved in the process, and DiJulio knew that from this point forward, a litigation-savvy filter would need to be applied to all future communication.

Concurrent with the creation of the appraisal and purchase offer, DiJulio crafted a three-point rejection of joint development with HTK and put an immediate halt to any meaningful discussions on the matter. SMP thanked HTK very much for their input but explained that SMP had a few problems with discussing a partnership with HTK at that time. First, they said the station design and size was still quite preliminary and would not be decided until the design, build, operate, and maintain (DBOM) contract with the builder of the monorail had been finalized, which was likely not to occur for a year or so. Second, they pointed out that they had made no definitive plans for either integrated or associated development at the site with anyone and did not intend to at this early stage. And third, they told HTK that they anticipated that the unnamed DBOM contractor would need flexibility and would likely need the unused property, *if any*, for construction staging, staff parking, and materials storage. SMP said they would be happy to speak with HTK about some associated development on the unused land, *if any*, in five years or so, but for the time being they were sorry—they had no alternative but to acquire the entire site. That was the official message on record.

Off the record, however, there was more to the story. SMP was concerned that the cost of a partial condemnation might exceed that of an entire taking. If SMP condemned only the station footprint portion of the property, the agency would have to pay HTK for the station footprint and lease the excess to be used for construction staging for an indeterminate period of years. It would also be liable for damages to the ground lessee, Rokan Partners, for demolishing the garage and its income stream. And SMP could also be liable for damages to Rokan's subtenant, Ampco Parking, which operated the parking operation and would suffer financial loss as well.

SMP was troubled by the three layers of property interests, because coming to an agreement with one party would be hard enough, but coming to an agreement with all three in some partial condemnation would be much more complicated since the interests of the three were not well aligned. In the unlikely event that SMP were able to come to some sort of agreement with all three parties, then SMP was dependent on each one actually doing what they said they would do. Frankly, the chances of that were not exactly shining, and the consequences to SMP of such an abrogation would be costly. The battle lines were drawn.

## JUSTIFYING A CONDEMNATION

Legally, a successful conclusion to a condemnation petition is conditioned upon the condemnor's ability to pass a three-pronged test used by the courts to evaluate eminent domain cases: the condemning authority must prove that (1) the use is indeed public, (2) the public interest requires it, and (3) the property appropriated is necessary for that use. While arguably there is some redundancy within the three components, these are the elements that no agency document, specification, or policy can conclusively contradict. An admission by DiJulio's troops that SMP didn't really need more than half the site at Boren's Block One could harpoon at least one prong of the legal test he would soon have to pass. DiJulio could not control what he saw as the mountain of evidence already out there, but he could easily dismiss any existing negative message as merely "preliminary" and then try to harness all the noise from that point forward.

HTK Management LLC employed the services of another prominent land-use firm in Seattle: Hillis, Clark, Martin, and Peterson (derisively known to the monorailiens as Hillis, Billus, and Killus).

Longtime Kubota family attorney Douglas Palmer Jr. (and a part-ner at Hillis, Clark, Martin, and Peterson) had close ties with the Japanese-American community, and he had handled the HTK ac-count for more than twenty years, albeit for most of those years he had been, ironically, with DiJulio's firm, Foster Pepper and Shefel-man. Palmer had met Henry Kubota in 1974 when the SHBC sold Kubota's home to Toshi Moriguchi, son of Fujimatsu and a college classmate of Palmer's. During this transaction, Palmer obviously im-pressed Kubota enough to land H. T.'s business after the falling out with Mimbu.

George Kresovich, the litigator at Hillis et al. that Palmer put in charge of the case, had simple marching orders from John Fujii: do your best to retain as much of the property as possible (absent the ground lease if possible) and ensure just compensation for any land condemned. Palmer's opening salvo focused on the associated devel-opment angle, deciding that if you can't beat them, join them.

As it turned out, developer William Justen, who was represent-ing the interests of the Pike Place Market station and the Smith Tower, seemed to be quite fond of publicity, especially the kind that enhanced either his project or persona; hence, each time he had even the slightest transit epiphany, it was as public as Paris Hilton's sex life. In the process of his negotiations, SMP policy and proce-dure were being rewritten with every development meeting he con-ducted; plus, he was telling everyone who would listen all about his conquests. And lots of folks were listening.

This new development paradigm was all the road map Palmer needed to achieve what his client desired, so in a preemptive strike made prior to the completion of the SMP appraisal in December 2003, Palmer offered to partner with SMP in the development of the site. The offer said they could have their station, and they could have their construction staging, but after it was all said and done, HTK would get whatever was left—sans the ground lease. To but-tress the offer, Palmer assembled a development team to meet with the SMP to discuss the opportunities for joint development on the site. The parties met three times but produced very little, because the SMP continually expressed their need and intent to acquire all the property for the purposes of locating the station and for demolition, staging, and construction activities. If that argument wasn't enough, they added that the designs were too preliminary for anything other than conceptual discussions.

On April 28, 2004, SMP attorney DiJulio filed a summons and complaint in the matter of the Petition of the Seattle Popular Monorail Authority, a city transportation authority, to acquire by condemnation certain real property, Second and Yesler station, for public use. The case schedule was set, a judge assigned, and respondent counsel Kresovich filed his notice of appearance. The trial date was set for December 20, 2004—a date too late for SMP's liking—so the petitioner sought to accelerate the proceedings, while HTK Management LLC concurrently began a strategy of trying to delay.

HTK made a motion to the court to continue a preliminary hearing set for June 11, 2004, due to the fact that it had been deprived of a number of critical things it needed in order to prepare for the hearing (read: blah, blah, blah). DiJulio objected and countered with a little blah, blah, blah of his own, offering a declaration of the SMP manager of special projects to detail exactly why the court could not allow such continuance. The manager of special projects (who, incidentally, was the individual hired specifically to manage the Pike Place Market project) identified herself in the declaration as the person "responsible for associated and integrated development at station locations along the Green Line" and chronicled a sequence of events that refuted the HTK arguments while substantiating the need for the SMP to have a speedy trial in order to facilitate possession of the property by October 1, 2004:

> Before recommendations on DBOM contractors can be made to the SMP's board for consideration, the SMP must be able to represent to the potential DBOM contractors that they will have access to every station property along the Green Line. If the SMP is not

able to grant access to any station along the Green Line alignment, and that property happens to be one of those on which the contractor needs to commence demolition immediately, the cost to SMP, and therefore the taxpayers, is $25,000 per day of delay.

Forget the fact that no DBOM contractor had submitted any offer yet nor would for three more months; forget the fact that SMP had imposed those penalties on itself in the request for proposals. What's important to remember is that SMP was in complete control of the time lines and, in their need for speed, had optimistically assumed that everything would follow a better-case scenario in the worst case.

Before the judge had a chance to rule on the HTK motion to continue, he de facto granted it by recusing himself from the matter entirely, which brought the proceedings to an abrupt halt. The smartest guy in the room, Judge Douglas McBroom, excused himself at more than one month into the trial and had the case reassigned. Good move. The next judge was even smarter—she unloaded the case from her docket in less than a week. Jeffrey M. Ramsdell, the judge who apparently drew the short straw, was bestowed with the honor of presiding over this messy affair—two months, two judges, and thirty-one filings into the matter. So everyone started over.

A new motion for an early trial date was made by SMP, which of course HTK vigorously opposed. Superior Court caseloads being what they are, Judge Ramsdell's schedule was not much better than the previous two judges' had been, and he noted the trial for December 20, 2004, but in doing so tossed a significant crumb to SMP: he would break the trial into two parts and schedule a hearing on the public use and necessity portion of the petition for August 23, 2004, just over one month away. The valuation phase of the trial, if needed, would be later. This consolation prize comforted SMP little, and DiJulio made a motion to reassign the case once again, to no avail.

## ESTABLISHING PUBLIC USE AND NECESSITY

The month before the manager of special projects had made her declaration (on June 11, 2004) in support of an early trial date, a new iteration of the design for the Pioneer Square station was completed, in May 2004. Shaped like a right triangle, the station now sat only at the eastern end of the site instead of covering the whole of Boren's Block One, with the hypotenuse traveling the length of Second Avenue and a longer upright leg running from the northeast corner of the site at Second and James to a point roughly one third down the southern property line on Yesler. The footprint of the station was about 6,500 square feet and covered less than a third of the property. The remainder of the property (which no longer showed a building on it) had written across it "construction staging, lay-down area for materials, staff and temporary parking."

SMP was wisely paring back the size and cost of its stations in the face of revenue shortfalls and was leaving behind some sizable chunks of land in the process. The Pioneer Square station was a still preliminary design, of course, they said, and an interesting one surely, since triangles as a form would seem to have questionable utility in a space destined for heavy pedestrian traffic. There was one benefit of the triangle, however, which was that the remainder parcel was now seemingly large enough to develop.

Being the good guys that they were, HTK Management LLC perhaps too reasonably agreed that the use—a monorail station and the construction staging area—were public uses and required for the construction of the Green Line. Fujii and his family wanted to cooperate but, in doing so, had summarily agreed that the first prong of the condemnation test—public use—had been satisfied. HTK pinned its argument on the notion that since the staging area was not a permanent use, then SMP did not need to condemn a permanent interest for that part of the site, only a temporary one. To that end, HTK and SMP entered a stipulation and order with the court on July 19, 2004, that documented the areas of agreement between the two, wherein HTK stipulated that the land under the station footprint and the right to use the remainder for construction staging during the construction period were both public uses and necessary for those uses.

## Proving No Constructive Fraud

DiJulio gladly accepted the gift of the first prong and went straight to work on the others, which involved asking the judge to preclude HTK from alleging any fraud on the part of SMP. To date, HTK had not suggested in any of its briefs that the petitioner had committed any fraudulent acts in the course of its efforts to condemn property along the Green Line, and DiJulio wanted to keep it that way. He filed his *motion in limine* three weeks before the August 23, 2004, public use and necessity hearing. This was a very important motion because, by preventing HTK from introducing evidence of fraud, SMP sought to undercut the only legitimate defense that DiJulio believed was available to HTK.

Remember that in the three-pronged test for a condemnation, the condemning authority must prove (1) the use is public, (2) the public interest requires it, and (3) the property appropriated is necessary for that use. In addressing the second and third prongs, DiJulio stated that generally accepted legal theory holds that only the first prong of this test is a judicial question that is subject to review by the courts; the second and third prongs are not judicial but legislative in nature, established by virtue of the enabling legislation.

DiJulio's argument was based on this: Provided a property owner cannot prove fraud on the part of the condemning authority or evidence of intentional acts so arbitrary and capricious so as to constitute constructive fraud, then the second and third prongs are deemed satisfied—the logic being that a judge should not have to divine whether or not a transit system needs nineteen stations to serve its public use. Reasonable people can have differing opinions as to whether nineteen stations are required and necessary for a monorail system—maybe seventeen or eighteen would suffice—thus case law has consistently supported the right of the condemning authority to decide the question. Article I, Section 16, of the Washington State Constitution doesn't place the burden upon a condemning authority of having to prove their methods in providing the public use, for which there may be more than one good answer.

Further, prior case law has consistently affirmed the concept that a condemning authority need not require the whole bundle of rights attendant with a fee interest for its public use to acquire those rights. For instance, very few public uses would require taking the mineral rights to a piece of property, but they are legally taken nonetheless. The simple fact that the legislation has mandated the taking is determinative, and hence the logic follows that the condemnor should be given great latitude in their good-faith conclusion as to necessity—with the sole caveat that there is no conduct that rises to the level of fraud.

The *motion in limine* was filed August 5, 2004, to prohibit HTK Management LLC from introducing any testimonial or documentary evidence of actual or constructive fraud on the part of SMP at the hearing on public use and necessity scheduled for August 23, 2004. DiJulio argued that the motion should be granted because (1) HTK had admitted that SMP had made no false representations to it regarding the decision to acquire the property by condemnation, and (2) HTK had no information that SMP intended to use the property for anything other than a public use. As authority, DiJulio referenced the deposition of John Fujii, wherein DiJulio induced him to parrot the two admissions, and a stipulated agreement between the parties, which detailed the HTK admission that the station and construction staging were both a public use and necessary for that use (HTK disputed only the necessity of acquiring a permanent fee interest for the staging area).

As icing on the cake, DiJulio cited the position that the determination of necessity is a legislative issue, which is deemed conclusive by the courts when found to exist by the appropriate legislative body, absent actual or constructive fraud. DiJulio was not only arguing his motion, he was handing the judge the rationale for granting the order of public use and necessity at the hearing to come on August 23rd.

In his brief opposing DiJulio's motion, HTK counsel Kresovich termed the maneuver a "summary judgment motion masquerading as a *motion in limine*." He rejected the legal notion that necessity was purely a legislative issue, while making a thinly veiled suggestion that some evidence of fraud might be discovered before the hearing on August 23rd. Kresovich offered some smoke in the form of a valuation study (sealed by protective order) commissioned by SMP that suggested SMP might be contemplating a sweetheart deal with the Smith Tower owner or another third party after the construction period.

Kresovich was correct in his estimation of the *motion in limine*, but his smoke had no fire. He knew he was in deep trouble. Realizing he needed to come up with something fast, he started obfuscating and making rapid-fire motions one after another. Needing some new information quickly, his first action was to file a motion to speed up the discovery phase of the trial and force SMP to expedite their responses to HTK requests for production of documents. He needed evidence of some questionable dealings that might rise to the level of constructive fraud, so he sought to unearth that mountain of evidence that DiJulio was doing his best to bury.

Next—eight days after the *motion in limine* was filed and four days before the judge would rule on it—Kresovich made three more motions. The first one was a motion to continue the public use and necessity hearing in order to buy some time. The second motion was to shorten the time for hearing the first motion to postpone the public use and necessity hearing, so as to give the judge time to rule on his third motion, which was to dismiss the whole case entirely, based on the argument that the court had no subject matter jurisdiction.

This third filing was a motion of desperation. From the beginning of our union, Americans have forever been distrustful of their government and its powers, especially when it comes to the taking of private property. As a result, constitutional safeguards had been installed to protect the general population from an overreaching government abusing its powers. With regard to the power of eminent domain, the courts have consistently held that when a government (in this case, the Washington State Legislature) grants eminent domain power to a lesser condemning authority (such as a county, a city, or a transit authority), it must explicitly prescribe the specific statutory procedure in the enabling legislation for the exercise of that power. In Washington State, counties, cities, and school districts all have slightly different procedures that they must follow in order to comply with the due process requirements of the state constitution.

Kresovich argued that the SMP was an entity known as a city transportation authority (which was specifically created for the monorail expansion), and its enabling legislation contained no specific reference to any condemnation procedure; therefore it was, according to Kresovich, flawed and fatally defective. Because of this defect, the superior court had no jurisdiction in the determination of public use and necessity, since SMP had not the authority to condemn in the first place—no subject matter jurisdiction, no case.

DiJulio countered the subject matter jurisdiction motion with a fifteen-page novel of his own, which essentially stated that the motion should be denied not only because another judge had already denied an identical motion in another SMP condemnation trial, but also because HTK had already recognized the court's jurisdiction and SMP's authority to condemn when HTK signed the stipulation and order of July 19, 2004, admitting the public use and necessity. Since it was a city transportation authority, DiJulio opined, it was reasonably implied that SMP would condemn pursuant to the same procedures applicable to cities.

During the eighteen-day period from the date of SMP's motion in limine to the scheduled date of the public use and necessity hearing, the court recorded fifty-seven filings from the parties—motions, declarations, opposition briefs, reply briefs, protective orders, and affidavits. The trial was fast becoming a test of wills and, more importantly, a demonstration of financial resources, as SMP displayed seemingly unlimited legal assets, while Lilliputian HTK refused to be intimidated by the goliath.

When the dust settled after all the motion commotion, HTK came out a five-time loser. The SMP motion in limine to exclude evidence of fraud was granted, and the HTK motion to dismiss due to lack of subject matter jurisdiction was denied. The minuscule victory for respondent HTK in the entire fracas was that a motion to shorten the time for consideration of another motion to compel SMP production of some documents—namely, the DBOM contractor's proposal—was granted. Small victory indeed. Fifty-seven filings later, the best Kresovich could do was win a motion on when to hear another motion (which he later lost). Things were sinking fast.

The Public Use and Necessity Hearing In Re the Matter of the Petition of the Seattle Popular Monorail Authority, Second and Yesler Station—originally scheduled for August 23, 2004—was held on September 13, 2004, in Judge Ramsdell's court. The cumulative arguments made and evidence offered in more than 130 filings on 531 pages entered into the court record over the previous four months were paraded before the court in the form of four witnesses and twenty-seven exhibits. Respective counsels DiJulio and Kresovich made their impassioned closing arguments, and then, in an instant, it was over. The order adjudicating public use and necessity was signed by Judge Ramsdell and entered into the King County Superior Court record.

HTK Management LLC, anticipating the loss with paperwork in hand, immediately appealed the decision to the appellate court. The appellate division passed on the opportunity to take a swing at this one—mostly because time was of the essence and constitutional issues were in question—and kicked it upstairs to the Supreme Court of Washington.

## Determining the Value of Boren's Block One

Noticeably disinterested thus far was lessee Rokan Partners, which didn't even bother to weigh in at the hearing. Neither did Ampco

Parking. While Kantor and his attorney certainly watched with interest as HTK struggled furiously against the taking, he was a winner in either event. Kantor knew he would be paid handsomely in the condemnation, thus the just compensation portion of the trial was all that interested him, which was now set for July 11, 2005, ten months hence. The greed and avarice portion of the proceedings were now at hand, and suddenly two new eager beavers enter the fray.

DiJulio wanted to stay out of this fracas as best he could, so he immediately made a motion to bifurcate the trial—that is, to separate the final portion of the condemnation proceedings into two separate trials: one to determine the value of the property as a whole (which would happen soon) and a second to allocate the proceeds among the three parties in interest (which he figured might never happen). SMP had a stake in the first part but absolutely no interest in the second.

No one much cared about the bifurcation except Kresovich, who blathered on about SMP time lines and its consistent failure to adhere to same in opposition to the motion. In the end, the judge resolved the matter in true Solomon-esque fashion: he denied the bifurcation but agreed to split the trial into two phases ... OK. One can only assume that the semantic parsing was clearly for the emotional benefit of HTK (which hadn't won a single battle of consequence yet), since the only difference between the two outcomes was that both matters would now stay in his court instead of the second phase being dumped on some other judge.

This was a ruling he would regret. Judge Ramsdell continued the trial four months and set the new date for the first phase of the trial, a jury trial, on April 25, 2005, adding "absent extraordinary circumstances, this court will not entertain any additional motions to alter the trial date." Everyone's patience was running thin.

The competition was fierce between the respective parties to hire the most pliable third-party professionals—appraisers, engineers, consultants—to justify the laughable sums they would be proposing as "just compensation" for the Sinking Ship Garage. The values invented by the parties ranged from $6 million to $11.9 million, and a meeting of the minds was nowhere in sight. SMP trotted out a structural engineer who declared the concrete jungle was structurally unsound and in need of multimillion-dollar renovation, while Rokan Partners and HTK compounded the income they were receiving from the property at very favorable capitalization rates.

The attorneys' jostling was now raised to a new level of insanity as the motions, depositions, and declarations got longer and pettier. Traps were laid and mines buried while every inch of ground was hotly contested. Quibbling over constitutional issues was one thing, but fighting over money ... that's another matter completely. Mediation was scheduled for March 21, 2005, but nobody was acting as if it would have any effect.

The posturing continued as March 21 came and went without an agreement, but the process must have had an effect on SMP, realizing that HTK made a very sympathetic victim and might fare well before a jury of its peers. The other parties all knew SMP would blink first, since it was the only one spending somebody else's money. And true to form, on April 7, SMP caved and reached a mediated settlement with parties in interest—HTK, Rokan, and Ampco—agreeing to pay $10.4 million for Boren's Block One.

HTK was pleased with the number (which was subject to a Supreme Court affirmation of the trial court ruling on public use and necessity), but Rokan and Ampco were drooling. They couldn't wait for the second phase of the trial, to divide up the dough.

## Allocating the Condemnation Proceeds

In the wake of settlement agreement, the parties had agreed to attempt mediation to allocate the condemnation award, said mediation to be completed by April 28, 2005. If mediation failed, then the second phase of the trial would begin.

HTK Management LLC believed Kantor would never willingly settle (absent an outrageous outcome such as the SMP payment), owing to the fact that Kantor seemed to operate under the belief that nothing helped his cause more than protracted litigation. Kantor was a lawyer—so he *understood* a lot more than he *knew*—and everyone should know that lawyers are a lot smarter than everybody else, especially when it comes to the law. If a layperson foolishly came to swim in his pond, they had better have a lot of guts and a lot of stamina, because they might be swimming a long time. A very successful career could be made manhandling adversaries with just such a philosophy.

Thus, Kresovich decided it best to attempt to enforce a provision contained within the ground lease, which was, in the event of the inability to agree on the allocation of any condemnation award, to submit to binding arbitration. On behalf of HTK, Kresovich made the motion on April 11, 2005, to compel Rokan Partners (and its subtenant, Ampco Parking) to submit to binding arbitration.

## AWAITING THE WASHINGTON SUPREME COURT RULING

While all this nonsense was going on, something really important was happening in Olympia, Washington. On March 17, 2005, the Supreme Court of the State of Washington heard oral argument in the Matter of the Petition of the Seattle Popular Monorail Authority, a city transportation authority, to acquire by condemnation certain real property for the Second and Yesler station. The whole gang was there. They cleaned up pretty well, with pressed suits and polished shoes, which offered no evidence of the mud and urine lavished upon said suits and shoes, respectively, over the last year.

The basics of the case were rehashed once more. HTK argued that the trial court had no subject matter jurisdiction, due to the absence of a specific condemnation procedure in the enabling legislation, and that SMP was unnecessarily condemning a greater interest than the public use required. SMP offered its evidence that the condemnation procedure could be reasonably implied from the statute and that the condemnee had stipulated that the proposed uses for the entire site were in fact public uses and that the determination of necessity was essentially a legislative question rather than a judicial one.

HTK countered that the 1998 convention center case had changed the standard of review in the determination of necessity when the court unsealed the Pandora's box of exclusive legislative authority and inserted the concept of a "footprint" to determine necessity, which required judicial scrutiny. In turn, SMP asserted that the cost to taxpayers of condemning interests as HTK suggested—a fee interest plus a construction easement for an undetermined number of years—exceeded the monies required to condemn the entire parcel, implying that financial criteria must be considered by a public agency when determining what interests are necessary to condemn.

Back and forth they went. And then they stopped. Seven months would pass before the Supreme Court ruled on the matter. It was a very quiet seven months, and the parties enjoyed the much-needed respite. The pendency of the Supreme Court ruling hung over everyone's heads like a guillotine—but there was another shoe yet to drop.

## THE DBOM CONTRACT AND SMP FINANCING

The monorail's MVET revenue shortfalls and construction cost overruns became harder and harder to ignore as the SMP plans crept closer and closer to reality. As the day of signing a contract for construction of the monorail approached, ideas such as shortening the Green Line and extending the maturity of the bonds to be retired by the MVET were bandied about in attempts to close the solvency gap. Luckily for Seattle's taxpayers, the 800-pound gorilla could no longer be ignored.

On June 20, 2005, Joel Horn and the monorail staff presented to the SMP board their recommended DBOM contract (with Cascadia Monorail Company LLC) and their financing plan (outlining how to pay for it). Two days later, the Washington State Treasurer released a statement to the press in which he lambasted the financing plan and urged the city of Seattle to withhold issuance of permits that would allow construction to begin. He took issue with the SMP's decision to seek forty-year bonds—instead of the twenty-five-year bonds used by the city and state on other government projects—explaining that he felt paying more than five times the construction value to finance a project "is totally ludicrous." He added that this unusual financing plan would lower the city and state bond ratings, which would increase the cost of doing business to any government entity within the state that needed to borrow money.

The media was littered with stories about the DBOM contract and the financing plan, and none of their observations were happy. The public confidence in the SMP's ability to deliver on its promises was called seriously into question, and dissent evolved into revolt. Ten days after Joel Horn made his board presentation, the SMP Finance Committee stated it would not approve the staff-proposed plan. More turbulence followed; within the week, the chair of the SMP board, Tom Weeks, the formerly popular former city councilman, and Horn, the never popular consultant turned developer, were accused of everything but high crimes and misdemeanors and forced to resign their positions.

The agency was in chaos. The SMP board decided to take quick and decisive action, and they did, in the form of what they creatively called an "Action Plan," which would basically take them back to square one to figure out how the hell they got into this mess and how the hell to get out. They hired a cadre of analysts, consultants, peer reviewers, and contractors to review every misstep the agency had taken to get to this point, all the while insisting there were no sacred cows. It was navel gazing on steroids, a textbook example of why conspiracy theorists continually allege that every bureaucratic agency is incompetent, immoral, stupid, or both. Luckily, not much time or money was wasted on the Action Plan due to events taking place outside the SMP.

Wanting another shot at finally slaying the elevated beast, the vocal anti-monorailiens called for a second no-confidence vote on the SMP (the first no-confidence vote—Initiative 83—was handily defeated in November 2004). One of the openly disaffected, Seattle Mayor Greg Nickels, stated he would not issue permits for the construction of the Green Line and called for the voters of Seattle to put an end to the madness. In response, SMP's Department of Too-Little-Too-Late immediately issued a scaled-back Green Line proposal and an updated financing plan in an effort to wax the waning public sentiment toward the project. It did not have the desired results.

## 2005: THE FIFTH MONORAIL VOTE

The outcome of the anger and apathy was Proposition No. 1, which would be submitted to the city's electorate on November 8, 2005. If approved, it would breathe life into the monorail plan. If rejected, the monorail was dead. The city bureaucrats, including the mayor, publicly declared that they would abide by the voters' decision, whatever it was, and the SMP board promised to "terminate the project as quickly as practicable in the event the proposition was defeated."

Just a few weeks prior to the election, on October 20, 2005, the state Supreme Court handed down its decision, upholding Judge Ramsdell's trial court ruling and affirming the determination of public use and necessity. Two of the nine justices dissented.

As a result of the Supreme Court's mandate, the matter of the petition of the Seattle Popular Monorail Authority to acquire by condemnation certain real property for the Second and Yesler station could now be officially concluded. Sitting on Judge Ramsdell's desk were the stipulation, findings of fact, and decree of appropriation, which, once all three were signed, would allow SMP to take title to Boren's Block One upon presentation of $10.4 million to the court clerk.

The judge had thirty days within which to act. He, of course, was well aware of the pending fifth and final vote on the monorail and had wisely decided that time was not of the essence. This matter was far too weighty to receive anything but deferral. If the proposition was rejected, then perhaps SMP would just go away and the status quo would be maintained—all things considered, an equitable outcome.

If the proposition was approved, then the wheels of progress could continue—another just result. And since no one was pressuring him to sign it, he didn't sign it.

While his nonaction was certainly taken in the name of justice, there also may have been a tinge of empathy for the Kubota heirs motivating him. For more than a year, HTK Management LLC had swum furiously in the face of an overwhelming tide, and perhaps the judge didn't want HTK to lose its land to a dragon that might be slain in two weeks. Ramsdell thought SMP may have been over-stepping legislative intent in its actions but sincerely believed it had the law on its side. He was a reluctant accomplice and wanted to find some equity for John Fujii if he could. This was a good deed—which of course would not go unpunished—and both he and HTK would regret it.

In the Revised Code of Washington, a section addresses the procedure in the event of a discontinuance or abandonment of condemnation proceedings. It provides that the condemning entity "may discontinue the proceedings ... by paying or depositing in court all taxable costs incurred by any parties to the proceedings up to the time of such discontinuance." In other words, if SMP did not complete the taking, it would be liable to the parties (HTK, Rokan, and Ampco) for their attorney fees, consultants, appraisers, and all costs incurred fighting the condemnation.

On November 8, 2005, Proposition No. 1 was rejected. The monorail was dead.

On November 18, SMP, the headless dragon decapitated by the election ten days before, filed a notice of presentation with the court, which let the world know that SMP intended to present the decree of appropriation for entry in Judge Ramsdell's court on December 2, 2005, despite the resounding defeat of Proposition No. 1. "Damn the torpedoes! We're hopping aboard the sinking ship anyway," the notice said, in effect, "and if you want to do anything about it, you better act fast."

Fujii was stunned. He couldn't believe it. SMP was out of business, yet it still wanted to proceed with the taking. Could they do this? After all that he had gone through, was he now about to lose his family legacy to an agency whose ship had sunk? Would he drown right next to an empty lifeboat?

## SMP Proceeds with Condemnation

After a brief period of disarray, Fujii regained his equilibrium. A meeting was called. SMP explained that they intended to purchase the property due to an alleged increase in value above and beyond the $10.4 million award, combined with a desire to avoid the costs associated with abandonment. However, because they were such good guys, DiJulio put forth an offer to the three parties—HTK, Rokan, and Ampco: if the big three were willing to waive any claim for fees and costs associated with the abandoned condemnation, SMP would not ask to enter the decree of appropriation, leaving title with the parties in possession.

HTK immediately agreed, but Rokan and Ampco balked. The two tenants wanted the condemnation to proceed so they could take their money and be done with it. They had wanted this from the beginning, and their position, given the $10.4 million award, certainly had not changed. The process of allocating the award would be good to them.

Fujii was obsessed with retaining this sorry lot and its miserable garage, so he racked his brain for a new strategy. Kresovich explained to Fujii that the chances were slim—maybe 10 percent—that SMP would ultimately be successful in completing the taking, since the public use had evaporated with the election. Fujii, given the fact that HTK had already agreed in writing that the use was public, felt Kresovich's 10 percent was too great a chance to take. He wasn't feeling lucky.

Alternatively, Fujii could call DiJulio's bluff, gambling that SMP would not want the negative publicity of another very public misdeed as the defunct agency tried to condemn property it knew it didn't need.

A third option would be for HTK to acquiesce to the taking and then try to repurchase the property, but Fujii was worried about Horn's old boss Justen, who had deeper pockets and a greater need for the garage (for Smith Tower tenant parking) than HTK did.

Hoping to eradicate all probability of losing the land, HTK made an offer to buy Rokan's and Ampco's leasehold interests for a price equal to what they would receive if the condemnation were completed. If they agreed, he could then accept DiJulio's offer and the condemnation would be abandoned. But they declined, citing tax reasons (condemnation proceeds are not taxable, but a sale to Fujii would be); however, the fact of the matter was that they liked their position now and didn't give a rip about anything or anybody else. Fujii felt backed into a corner.

## HTK Proffers a Settlement

After many desperate and devious hours, HTK attorney Douglas Palmer Jr. came up with a plan. SMP had sought to condemn a good portion of the property for what would eventually become a private use, hadn't they? Associated development was defined as a sale of condemned land to a private party, wasn't it? Now SMP was going to proceed with a condemnation for which there was no longer a public use, correct? "Well, if they can do it, so can we!" went Palmer's line of reasoning. "Eureka! We can buy SMP's right to condemn!"

This brainstorm led to the execution of a document known as the Settlement, Indemnification and Assignment of Judgment Agreement. The settlement portion referred to the resolution of all outstanding issues between the two parties; the indemnification portion ensured that HTK would assume any and all SMP liability incurred as a result of the condemnation and/or its abandonment; and the assignment of judgment portion transferred all SMP's rights and interest in the property to HTK. The newest and strangest bedfellows in town, SMP and HTK, struck a deal whereby HTK would assume any potential SMP liability as a result of the whole mess in return for SMP assigning its right to condemn the property to HTK. What a concept—a property owner condemning his own property!

HTK would argue that they were forced to make this deal with SMP if they wanted to ensure title to Boren's Block One, but surely the idea of finally getting rid of the ground lease and Kantor was too tempting to ignore. The SMP board passed a resolution approving the deal, and the notice of assignment was filed with the court on December 14, 2005—and a new round of nonsense began.

## ROKAN AND AMPCO OBJECT

Inexplicably, Rokan Partners and Ampco Parking did a full 180-degree about-face. Furious that they had been outmaneuvered, they filed a forest's worth of papers condemning not only SMP's proposed condemnation (for the first time) but also the assignment agreement with HTK.

Because the public use upon which the taking was based had been terminated at the voter's box, they argued that SMP's continued right to condemn should also be vacated. Further, they said the assignment agreement should be found invalid for many reasons, the most important being the fact that the condemned interest was to be transferred to a private party that had no statutory power of eminent domain.

Their arguments were so crisp and impassioned that Kresovich wondered where they had been all that time when he had needed them. Ironically, they were promoting the precise notion that HTK had been futilely arguing all along—that is, a public agency wielding the power of eminent domain should not be able to transfer a condemned interest to a private party, immediately or otherwise—and SMP, which had been willing to do it once (through the associated development vehicle), certainly had no problem doing it again.

HTK, now with its SMP hat on, was strangely parroting DiJulio that public use and necessity had been stipulated by the parties, adjudged by the trial court, and affirmed by the Supreme Court. There was no going back, that train had already left the station. Rokan Partners, which had been tacitly advancing SMP's cause from the beginning, suddenly objected strenuously and wanted to stop the taking in favor of some inflated abandonment damages. Everyone was changing hats and positions so fast, it was hard to keep straight what the arguments were and who was making them.

The chaotic nature of the fracas only substantiated SMP's original desire to condemn the entire interest in the first place. HTK, Rokan, and Ampco had such supremely divergent interests and negotiating styles that forging an agreement with the three parties was a practical impossibility. The layering of interests—the fee, which was subject to the Rokan Partners ground lease, which was subject to the Ampco Parking sublease—only complicated matters to a ridiculous degree.

The hearing to entertain the motion brought by Rokan and Ampco to dismiss the condemnation and award attorney fees was heard on March 10, 2006. Rokan argued that HTK couldn't enter the stipulation and decree because HTK, as a private party, had no power of eminent domain and could not complete a condemnation action. Further, they noted that the assignment to HTK constituted constructive abandonment and as such entitled Rokan and Ampco to costs and attorney fees.

The arguments put forward in response by Kresovich, who was on crutches due to a skiing accident, were the same ones DiJulio had been forwarding for two years—and were as crippled as Kresovich's appearance suggested, because he was now making the same case that he had been ridiculing for nearly two years. All his blows were alligator punches, which were pulled so he would not sound like a hypocrite.

It was a bizarre scene, with DiJulio and Kresovich huddled together like sled dogs in a blizzard. Boiled down, the thrust of Kresovich's case was pleading with the court to exercise its use of equitable powers, since no one would be arguing about fees were it not for HTK's continued efforts to fight the taking. There was no injured party as a result of the assignment, so Kresovich felt the law need not concern itself with the details. The other condemned parcels along the Green Line would soon be sold to private parties, so what was wrong with agreeing to do so in advance in the interest of saving some taxpayer money?

Kresovich noted that SMP would be taking title to the property prior to assigning it to HTK, thus any tax implications to Rokan or Ampco were not at issue (although the language in the assignment agreement contemplated HTK entering the decree of appropriation and paying the money). Kresovich explained that Fujii had exhausted every legal means at his disposal to ensure retention of the property but was rebuffed at every turn. HTK had tried to give Rokan Partners what it said it wanted—a share of the $10.4 million—but now Kantor had changed his mind and wanted something he wouldn't have gotten: attorney fees (which wasn't entirely true, since the $10.4 million award supposedly included all attorney fees).

First, Kresovich begged the judge for a total victory. Then he begged for at least a partial victory by denying Rokan's motion for fees. And then he just begged.

## MAKING SENSE OF THE JUDGE'S RULING

After just two hours of argument, the judge issued his ruling, dismissing the condemnation action, vacating the decree of appropriation, and awarding Rokan and Ampco their costs and fees. All that was left standing from the Settlement, Indemnification and Assignment of Judgment Agreement was the HTK indemnification of SMP—the worst possible outcome for HTK.

While this ruling made more sense than had the original finding of public use and necessity, the nature and significance of a temporary public use would seem to need some clarification; Ramsdell had used the exact same rationale to originally permit the taking for a temporary use as he did to declare the assignment an abandonment. Whether the transfer to a private party occurred after a few hours (in the assignment), a few months (in the case of the other SMP-condemned properties), or a few years (with associated development) would seem to make little difference when applying common sense to understanding what is and what is not a temporary use.

Although competent jurists might argue that the difference was the application of a legislative standard of necessity versus a judicial one, nonetheless the law was not applied equally going in as it was coming out. Perhaps this is the rule of law, or perhaps the name of the respondent made the difference. While HTK could have argued that the assignment served a public purpose—as it saved the taxpayers the cost of abandonment—Kresovich did not. Since neither Rokan nor Ampco was damaged in any way by the assignment, the equitable powers argument held some sway; however, the judge was not able to make the considerable leap to knowingly permitting a private party to condemn another private party's interest.

HTK, however, was not deterred and indicated they would appeal again.

## AWARDING ATTORNEY FEES

Meanwhile, the sharks—Rokan Partners and Ampco Parking—filed motions to receive judgments for their "reasonable attorney fees," which over the course of their gnatlike attention span on the case had arrived at $294,488 and $311,781, respectively (by contrast, SMP's total legal bill was $312,892, while HTK lavished Kresovich, Palmer et al. with $598,000). No longer DiJulio's problem, this liability was now the burden of HTK, earned by virtue of the fabulous Settlement, Indemnification and Assignment of Judgment Agreement they had signed just months before.

To soften the blow, Kresovich fought the awards the tenants sought by arguing that most of the fees were spent on activities not reimbursable under the statute. He said they had not participated in the public use and necessity portion of the trial before the lower court or Supreme Court, that legal fees related to the allocation of the $10.4 million award were not contemplated in the abandonment statute, and that their attorney fees were, in a word, unreasonable.

Kresovich also grasped at the equitable powers straw again, noting that no one would be here fighting over fees had not HTK taken the issue to the Supreme Court, as the property would have been taken months ago like so many others.

The courtroom digressed into a third-grade playground; Rokan hurled insults while Kresovich covered his ears, stomped his feet, and made loud noises. To no one's surprise but maybe Kresovich's, he actually won something, as the fees to Rokan and Ampco were rightfully reduced more than $100,000 and $64,000, respectively. At long last, in the matter of the petition of the Seattle Popular Monorail Authority to condemn certain real property, Hillus, Billus, and Killus had finally prevailed.

A month later, the attorney for Rokan Partners filed a notice of withdrawal from the case (without substitution) and at the same time filed a lien for nonpayment of legal fees against his former client and its judgment. Apparently, Kantor had decided that the $100,000 in fees that were disallowed by the judge need not be paid. His decision notwithstanding, the lawyers were eventually paid anyway. Lawyers are good at that—getting paid, that is.

## 2007: An Unappealing Appeal ... and HTK Purchases the Leasehold Interest

As of Memorial Day 2007, the HTK appeal of Ramsdell's ruling in the assignment matter was not moving; both parties seemed to be suffering from legal fatigue. Ampco Parking still managed the Sinking Ship Garage; Kantor, now a sculptor living in Sun Valley, Idaho, enjoyed continued profit; and SMP was nothing but a punch line.

Fujii pondered the possibilities. His prospects for success in the higher courts were rightfully dampened by recent experience. He had lost every step of the way to this point, and he held far less conviction for the arguments he was now being forced to make (since they were, for all intents, the SMP arguments) than he held his first time through the ringer.

Fujii was left with one last option. Over the years, periodic discussions had been held concerning the acquisition of the lease-hold—always without success. But in the summer of 2007, something changed. For whatever reason, the newly minted sculptor—no longer with other property interests in Pioneer Square, with little hope of a fat condemnation award, and perhaps wanting to trade for some property with more relevance to his current life—apparently found this dangling participle at least as much an annoyance as an asset.

The discussions took on a new tone as the interests of the two adversaries now had more in common than at any time in years past. A price was quickly negotiated, and the purchase of Rokan Partner's leasehold interest by members of H. T. Kubota's extended family closed midyear in 2007. It was an all-cash deal, and the parties signed a confidentiality agreement to keep this once very public matter private.

After more than four decades, the ownership of the land and the garage improvements on Boren's Block One were now finally rejoined. The second generation of the Kubota family had finally extinguished the long-standing encumbrance and at long last were permitted quiet enjoyment of the troubled parcel.

To the casual observer today, nothing appears to have changed. The Sinking Ship Garage is still there and is still an eyesore, but another chapter in this story remains to be written. The descendants of Takemitsu Kubota will surely one day chart their own course and build their dreams atop the rubble of this sinking ship, but what will really change? Will they fare any better than those who came before them on this sorry and cursed lot?

# Epilogue:

# ACCEPTANCE

Boren's Block One, that seemingly insignificant molehill just east of the sag at the foot of what we know today as Yesler Way, had begun as a small fishing camp of the Duwampsh. Since the day this triangular plot of land was carved from the surrounding woods and given its name, a succession of good men have built their mountains upon it, only to bear witness to the perfect cruelty of gravity on their imperfect constructs.

Gravity's pull *was* a little stronger there.

When Chief Seattle, he of broad shoulders and regal bearing, rose to stand and deliver his most famous oration, he stood near that sag at the foot of Yesler Way. The year was 1854, and the little fishing camp was gone. The December rains had dampened the spirits of all the multitudes gathered save the eloquent chief. Gravity did not seem to exert its power over him; instead, he wore gravitas like a cedar cape. He towered above the surrounding crowd and, most conspicuously, the Governor of Washington Territory, five-foot-six-inch Isaac Stevens, for whom the convocation had been called.

Stevens, also the territorial Commissioner of Indian Affairs, arrived in town to present his treaty that he would soon impose upon the native Duwampsh tribe. He orchestrated a grand reception in his own honor. The shoreline was littered with hundreds of bobbing canoes and their bowlegged pilots, who had gathered to hear Chief Seattle—not Stevens—speak to the treaty. It was to be a speech that marked the tragic end of an era and a great nation, as well as the hopeful beginning of a town and a new culture. One form exchanged for another.

The great chief could clearly see what the future held, and he calmly accepted the hopelessness of his situation in hopes of relieving others of theirs. Dr. Hiram Smith, the namesake of Smith's Cove at the north end of Elliott Bay, and a grand admirer of the chief, was in attendance and recorded the events that followed:

> The governor was then introduced to the native multitude by Dr. Maynard and at once commenced in a conversational, plain, and straightforward style an explanation of his mission among them. When he sat down Chief Seattle arose with all the dignity of a senator who carries the responsibility of a nation on his shoulders. Placing one hand on the governor's head and slowly pointing heavenward with the index finger of the other, he commenced his memorable address in solemn and impressive tones. Neither his eloquence, his dignity nor his grace were acquired.

Chief Seattle, who refused to use the hybrid Chinook language that had evolved during the paleface invasion, spoke in his native Duwampsh:

> Yonder sky that has wept tears of compassion upon my people for centuries untold, and which to us appears changeless and eternal, may change. Today is fair. Tomorrow, it may be overcast with clouds. My words are like the stars that never change. Whatever Seattle says, the great chief at Washington can rely upon with as much certainty as he can upon the return of the sun or the seasons. The White Chief says the Big Chief at Washington sends us greetings of friendship and goodwill. This is kind of him for we know he has little need of our friendship in return. His people are many. They are the grass that covers vast prairies. My people are few. They resemble the scattering trees of a storm-swept plain. The great—and I presume good—White Chief sends us word that he wishes to buy our lands but is willing to allow us enough to live comfortably. This indeed appears just, even generous, for the Red Man no longer has rights that he need respect, and the offer may be wise also, as we are no longer in need of an extensive country.

There was a time when our people covered the land as the waves of a wind-ruffled sea cover its shell-paved floor, but that time long since passed away with the greatness of tribes that are now but a mournful memory. I will not dwell on, nor mourn over, our untimely decay, nor reproach my paleface brothers with hastening it as we too may have been somewhat to blame.

Youth is impulsive. When our young men grow angry at some real or imaginary wrong, and disfigure their faces with black paint, it denotes that their hearts are black, and that they are often cruel and relentless, and our old men and old women are unable to restrain them. Thus it has ever been. Thus it was when the white men first began to push our forefathers further westward. But let us hope that the hostilities between us may never return. We would have everything to lose and nothing to gain. Revenge by young men is considered gain, even at the cost of their own lives, but old men who stay behind at home in times of war, and mothers who have sons to lose, know better...

To us the ashes of our ancestors are sacred and their resting place is hallowed ground. You wander far from the graves of your ancestors and seemingly without regret. Your religion was written upon tables of stone by the iron finger of your God so that you could not forget. The Red Man could never comprehend nor remember it. Our religion is the traditions of our ancestors; the dreams of our old men, given them in the solemn hours of night by the Great Spirit; and the visions of our sachems; and is written in the hearts of our people.

Your dead cease to love you and the land of their nativity as soon as they pass the portals of the tomb and wander way beyond the stars. Our dead never forget the beautiful world that gave them being. They love its verdant valleys, its murmuring rivers, its magnificent mountains, sequestered valleys and tree-lined lakes and bays, and ever yearn in tender, fond affection over the lonely hearted living, and often return from the Happy Hunting Ground to visit, guide, console, and comfort them.

Day and night cannot dwell together. The Red Man has ever fled the approach of the White Man as the morning mist flees before the morning sun.

However, your proposition seems fair and I think my people will accept it and retire to the reservation you offer them. Then we will dwell apart in peace, for the words of the Great White Chief seem to be the words of nature speaking to my people out of the dense darkness.

It matters little where we pass the remnant of our days. They will not be many. The Indians' night promises to be dark. Not a single star of hope hovers over his horizon. Sad-voiced winds moan in the distance. Grim Fate seems to be on the Red Man's trail, and wherever he goes he will hear the approaching footsteps of his fell destroyer and prepare stolidly to meet his doom, as does the wounded doe that hears the approaching footsteps of the hunter.

A few more moons, a few more winters—and not one of the mighty hosts that once moved over this broad land or lived in happy homes protected by the Great Spirit will remain to mourn over the graves of a people once more powerful and hopeful than yours. But why should I mourn at the untimely fate of my people? Tribe follows tribe, and nation follows nation, like the waves of the sea. It is the order of nature, and regret is useless. Your time of decay may be distant, but it will surely come, for even the White Man whose God walked and talked with him as friend with friend cannot be exempt from the common destiny. We may be brothers after all. We will see.

We will ponder your proposition, and when we decide we will let you know. But should we accept it, I here and now make this condition that we will not be denied the privilege without molestation of visiting at any time the tombs of our ancestors, friends, and children. Every part of this soil is sacred in the estimation of my people. Every hillside, every valley, every plain and grove has been hallowed by some sad or happy event in the days long vanished. Even the rocks, which seem to be dumb and dead as they swelter in the sun along the silent shore, thrill with memories of stirring events connected with the lives of my people, and the very dust upon which you now stand responds more lovingly to their footsteps than to yours because it is rich with the blood of our ancestors, and our bare feet are conscious of the sympathetic touch. Our departed braves, fond mothers, glad, happy-hearted maidens, and even the little children who lived here and rejoiced here for a brief season will love these somber solitudes, and at eventide they greet shadowy returning spirits. And when the last Red Man shall have perished and the memory of my tribe shall have become a myth among the White Men, these shores will swarm with the invisible dead of my tribe, and when your children's children think themselves alone in the field, the store, the shop, upon the road, or in the silence of the pathless woods, they will not be alone. In all the earth there is no place dedicated to solitude. At night when the streets of your cities and villages are silent and you think them deserted, they will throng with the returning hosts that once filled them and still love this beautiful land. The White Man will never be alone.

Let him be just and deal kindly with my people, for the dead are not powerless. Dead, did I say? There is no death, only a change of worlds.

The lands of the Duwampsh became the city of Seattle, and the small fishing camp just east of the sag at the foot of Yesler Way became Boren's Block One. The departed forefathers of Chief Seattle, faithful stewards of the land—and the little fish camp—are not alone. At eventide, they have more company now, and I suspect there are more shadowy souls yet to arrive.

# ACKNOWLEDGMENTS

Many hands make light work and I have enjoyed a village-full of hands in this project, which is good news since, for this author, it takes a whole library to make a book.

My primary expression of gratitude goes to John Fujii, whose candor, generosity, and patience seemingly know no bounds. Without his help, the complete telling of this story would not have been possible. I would also like to thank Greg Lange, the Suzuki family, and all of the folks named in the book who graciously shared their time and their experience so I could add color to the previously dark parts of the narrative. On the production side, praise goes to Lori Fulsaas, Tom Griffin, Meryl Schenker, Chris Fraser, and especially Kris Fulsaas. Kris is my literary savior, possessing a broad knowledge of all the relevant trivia about which I, sadly, have no clue. Thank you all.

# Suggested Reading

**Bagley, Clarence B.** *History of Seattle.* 3 vols. Chicago: S. J. Clarke Publishing Company, 1916.

**Broderick, Henry.** *Early Seattle Profiles.* Seattle: Dogwood Press, 1959.

**Denny, Arthur A.** *Pioneer Days on Puget Sound.* Seattle: The Alice Harriman Company, 1908.

**Denny, Emily Inez.** *Blazing the Way.* Seattle: Rainier Printing Company, 1909.

**Ichioka, Yuji.** *The Issei: The World of the First Generation Japanese Immigrants 1885—1924.* New York: The Free Press, 1988.

**Ito, Kazuo.** *Issei, a History of Japanese Immigrants in North America.* Translated by Shinichiro Nakamura and Jean S. Gerard. Seattle: Japanese Community Service (1414 South Weller Street, Seattle, WA 98144), 1973.

**Jones, Nard.** *Seattle.* Garden City, NY: Doubleday and Company, 1972.

**King County.** Real Property Archives, Seattle.

**Morgan, Murray.** *Skid Road.* New York: Ballantine Books, 1971.

**Newell, Gordon.** *Totem Tales of Old Seattle.* New York: Superior Publishing Company, 1956.

**Sone, Monica.** *Nisei Daughter.* Seattle: University Washington Press, 1953.

**Speidel, Bill.** *Doc Maynard, the Man Who Invented Seattle.* Seattle: Nettle Creek Publishing Company, 1978.

**State of Washington.** Puget Sound Regional Archives. Bellevue, WA.

**Takami, David A.** *Divided Destiny.* Seattle: University of Washington Press and Wing Luke Asian Museum, 1998.

**Watt, Roberta Frye.** *Four Wagons West.* Portland, OR: Binford and Mort Publishing, 1931.

Made in the USA
Lexington, KY
13 April 2010